Monetary Whispers Across Space

Iwan J. Azis

Monetary Whispers Across Space

Springer

Iwan J. Azis
Dyson School of Applied Economics
Cornell University
Ithaca, NY, USA

ISBN 978-981-95-4624-4 ISBN 978-981-95-4625-1 (eBook)
https://doi.org/10.1007/978-981-95-4625-1

This work was supported by Bank Indonesia Institute.

This Springer imprint is published by the registered company Springer Nature Singapore Pte Ltd.
The registered company address is: 152 Beach Road, #21-01/04 Gateway East, Singapore 189721, Singapore

Foreword

A nation's economic vitality is not forged in the boardrooms of its largest corporations alone, but in the aspirations and endeavors of its people across every island and valley. It is also too naive to assume that policymakers know everything. Indonesia's story of robust national growth is a testament to its potential, yet this narrative of success often masks the persistent inequalities that fragment our archipelago. While macroeconomic indicators may paint a picture of stability, a closer look reveals a concentration of economic power and opportunity, predominantly within Java, leaving peripheral regions, especially in the east, trailing in its wake.

This reality presents a profound challenge: to ensure that the currents of prosperity reach every shore. It is a challenge that cannot be met with monolithic policies crafted from a national vantage point. The diverse tapestry of Indonesia's regional economies, each with its unique structural and institutional fabric, demands a more nuanced and responsive approach. A one-size-fits-all solution is not merely ineffective; it is an injustice to the distinct potential of each region.

The path forward requires us to listen—to truly hear the "monetary whispers across space." We must build bridges of understanding between central policymakers and the realities on the ground. This means establishing robust systems for regional data collection and fostering genuine partnerships with local governments and financial institutions. These are not just technical exercises; they are the foundations of a more sensitive and effective policy framework.

This book, *Monetary Whispers across Space*, courageously steps into this complex arena. It moves beyond aggregate numbers to explore the intricate dance between monetary policy and regional disparity. With a sharp focus on the pivotal role of local credit, it illuminates how the flow of capital can both entrench and alleviate inequality. Through a blend of rigorous empirical analysis and the vital perspectives of regional financial actors, this work provides the insights needed to craft policies that are not only context-sensitive but truly transformative.

Let this work be a call for more and better actions. It is a reminder to policymakers that the effectiveness of their decisions is intrinsically linked to the diverse economic landscapes they seek to shape or reshape. It underscores the critical need for collaboration—unified efforts among central and local authorities, financial institutions, and the communities themselves. Our goal must be not only to stimulate growth but also to cultivate a future where that growth is shared, fostering equitable and inclusive prosperity across the entirety of our beloved Indonesia. By embracing the lessons within these pages, we can design policies that are more precise, more impactful, and more just, ensuring that every region has the opportunity to flourish.

Jakarta, Indonesia
June 2025

Perry Warjiyo
Governor of Bank Indonesia

Preface

It all began with the research program on two dimensions of dualism and inequality, i.e., between regions and between small and large businesses. That program led to the publication of *Periphery and Small Ones Matter* (Springer, 2022), the key proposition of which was for social planners to avoid making policies not compatible with the prevailing social capital in the regions. Once completed, a more detailed analysis was requested, particularly on the policy implications of it. However, conducting a detailed analysis on two dimensions of inequality at the same time is extremely difficult, especially if specific policy measures are expected to emerge from the analysis. Wisely, it was decided to break the research program into two parts: one is to focus on dualism between micro-small medium enterprises (MSME) and large businesses, and another is to focus on inequality between regions. The first part was completed last year and was reported in the *Listen and Design* (Springer 2024). The current book is intended to report on the second part.

In the spirit of blending macro-policy analysis (monetary policy in particular) with regional development perspectives, here I wish to emphasize the concerning trend of inequality between regions, and how national monetary policy designed for macroeconomic stability interacts with such a trend. Hence, the book is about how monetary decisions intersect with geography.

I am grateful to Bank Indonesia (BI), especially Bank Indonesia Institute (BINS), for giving me the opportunity to explore in more detail a topic that I am deeply interested in and have strong feelings about. I firmly believe that the issue of interregional inequality is very important for a country like Indonesia, the world's largest archipelago. To the extent that the country's inequality between regions is the highest among countries of comparable size, it is also my conviction that many development policies are, in one way or another, interconnected with this inequality. The issue should be inseparable from broader development programs or policies and cannot be treated in isolation. In this context, the main hypothesis that I chose to advance in this book is that there is a two-way relationship between monetary policy and interregional inequality. Central to the analysis are the heterogeneous responses of different regions to national monetary policy.

The analysis inevitably highlights the interactions between macro- and micro-developments. Since the macro part (monetary policy) and the micro part (interregional inequality) occupy distinct domains, where each is governed by its own dynamics and principles, many argue that the two should be analyzed separately, not in a single-mechanism system. I reject this argument. I challenge the notion that monetary policy and interregional inequality are not connected. Our analysis suggests that the associations between monetary policy and interregional inequality are not merely based on chance. The underlying assumptions and mechanisms on how monetary policy is impacting regional development play a critical role in uncovering the ways in which the two actually interact. From the policy perspective, understanding such interactions enables one to better align macro-level objectives (growth, inflation, employment) with the urgent need to foster equitable development and balanced spatial development.

I would like to thank Dr. Perry Warjiyo, the Governor of Bank Indonesia (BI), for his continued support to my research through BINS, and to Destry Damayanti, MSc, the Senior Deputy Governor of BI, Dr. Juda Agung and Doni P. Joewono, MBA, the Deputy Governors of BI, for their encouragement to conduct research on this particular topic. I greatly benefited from the help and assistance of BINS under the leadership of the former head, Dr. Yoga Affandi, who contributed his thoughts and suggestions, especially at the early stage of research framework development. I also thank the current head of BINS, Clarita Gaya Iskandar MIA, and the research director, Dr. Cicilia Anggadewi Harun for their continued encouragement. I cannot thank them and their staff enough for making my work run smoothly.

I am particularly grateful to the Bank Indonesia Regional Offices (KPw) for their tremendous help during our field research. All field surveys were made easier thanks to their excellent coordination and the work of KPw consultants. The discussions and conversations with local banks, including the association of the small bank's head, Tedy Alamsyah, local businesses, academics, local communities, and regional government offices in Aceh, Papua, and other regions, gave a lot of nuances to the quantitative results of the formal surveys, which I really appreciate. Without such nuances, the results of the questionnaires would have been dry and lacking true inside stories that help guide our conclusions and policy recommendations.

Some BINS leadership and researchers who accompanied me in field surveys, Yoga Affandi, Cicilia Anggadewi Harun, M. Cahyaningtyas, Danny Hermawan, Rizky Fitrama, Arnita Rishanty, and Shinta Fitrianti, helped improve the quality of the survey through their questions and arguments during the discussions. I thank them for their valuable contributions. For the research work itself, I am grateful to have members of a research team in my corner under the effective coordination of Arnita Rishanty, who basically managed everything behind the scenes, allowing me to believe that things are "under control." The members of my very capable research team are Hardy Salim, Wan Hasjim Omar Jacob Saleh, and Rahmat Esar Salsabil. Toward the completion of research reporting, we also received help from Meita Rosa Indah and two BINS research assistants, Misbahol Yaqin and Naufal Alfaraby Winandita, for which I am very grateful.

I also would like to express my sincere gratitude to my dear friends, Fawzy Siddik and Ralph Christy, who accompanied me in some of the field surveys, not only for their advice and directions but also for making the trips fun and exciting. My heartfelt thanks also go to Hayley Hughes for graciously allowing me to seclude myself in her charming cottage in Austin, Texas, during the final stretch of writing this book.

I am profoundly blessed to be embraced by the love and encouragement of my two children, Mirko and Mariko, whose presence fills my life with joy and purpose. To my wife, Erina, whose unwavering support and constant reminder to "think beyond the obvious" continue to challenge and inspire me, I am deeply indebted.

Ithaca, NY, USA
April 2025

Iwan J. Azis

Contents

List of Figures

List of Tables

Chapter 1
Introduction

Decades ago, most regions outside Jawa and those in Eastern Indonesia stood as a stark symbol of less-developed parts of Indonesia. At the time, outside Jawa faced greater infrastructure deficiencies than Jawa. The disparities between regions were glaring, with income, wealth, and opportunities concentrated in Jawa. Any measures of interregional inequality confirmed the observation.

Today, decades later, many of the same regions outside of Jawa and eastern Indonesia remain less developed compared to Jawa-Bali. Despite the significant strides made in overarching economic growth and national achievements, and certain areas have exhibited signs of increased prosperity, many regions continue to struggle economically. Some are still entrenched in poverty and others in stagnation as the promises of progress have failed to materialize.

Over the years, a myriad of policies have been implemented. The country's macro conditions improved, showing resilience and steady progress, marked by sustained growth in GDP and declining poverty rates. Even in bad times, including during the COVID-19 pandemic, Indonesia managed to maintain relative stability, with inflation largely under control and a prudent fiscal framework kept the debt levels manageable. Some of those policies, implicitly or explicitly, were also expected to bridge the gaps between Jawa and non-Jawa, to foster more balanced development.

It feels as though macro-level advancements have failed to penetrate the fabric of grassroots development and capture the gap between developed and less-developed regions, leaving many local communities untouched by progress. The very mechanisms designed to reduce the gap have either faltered in implementation or been insufficient to counter the forces perpetuating regional disparity. The disconnect between macro-level success and micro-regional level struggles reflects a troubling oversight, highlighting a critical imbalance that underscores the need for more inclusive and equitable development strategies.

Given such circumstances, it is crucial to examine the prevailing macroeconomic strategies and policies by scrutinizing their underlying assumptions, mechanisms, and regional impact to uncover the ways in which these policies fail to address

I. J. Azis, *Monetary Whispers Across Space*,
https://doi.org/10.1007/978-981-95-4625-1_1

interregional inequality. This is the background thinking behind the writing of this book. Our goal is to improve the conduct of macro-policy to better align macro-level objectives with the urgent need to foster equitable development and balanced spatial development. In the current volume, the macropolicy we focus on is monetary policy, particularly its influence on credit allocation at the regional level, and the heterogeneous responses to the policy that have implications for interregional inequality.

Indonesia's monetary policy has faced challenges in effectively meeting multiple targets to maintain growth, price stability, and financial stability at the same time. Although inequality between regions may not be on the agenda, Bank Indonesia (BI) has been keen to strengthen the operations of its regional offices (currently there are 46 of such offices) to support BI's functions at the regional level. Their tasks include controlling local inflation, monitoring regional economies, disseminating, communicating and implementing BI's policies, engaging with local stakeholders, and collecting and analyzing regional economic and financial data to support decision-making and policy formulation. The analysis in this book aligns closely with several of these tasks, particularly as it examines the heterogeneous responses of different regions to national monetary policy. By highlighting the distinct impacts of monetary policy on regional development, the analysis sheds light on the dynamics that contribute to persistent disparities between regions, ultimately shaping the broader pattern of interregional inequality.

One of the most pivotal regional variables intrinsically linked to national monetary policy is regional credit. The extent of its allocation in each region not only reflects regional economic conditions but also plays a significant role in shaping how monetary policy impacts local development trajectories. From this perspective, the role of local banks as the main agent of credit allocation is critical. The behavior that reflects their liquidity preference and their response to any changes in monetary policy play a pivotal role in fostering economic growth and stability within their regions. The ability of local banks to assess regional conditions, risks, and opportunities allows for a more responsive and effective credit allocation, directly affecting local development and job creation. Through credit allocation, they act as crucial intermediaries between national monetary policies and regional economic realities, and serve as a bridge ensuring that the benefits of national monetary policy extend to even the most localized economic landscapes. For this reason, local banks were selected as the main group of respondents to our questionnaires, where the primary focus was on the local bank's priorities, the key performance indicator (KPI), and the course of actions they are taking with respect to liquidity preference and credit allocation.

Indonesia's credit-to-GDP ratio is notably low, only around 32%, which is the lowest among six Southeast Asian countries; per 2023, Thailand's ratio stood at 119.13%, Malaysia at 117.16%, the Philippines at 48.3%, Cambodia at 173.37% and Brunei at 35.79%. Low financial inclusion (about half of Indonesia's population lacks bank accounts), the relatively small size of the banking system, and super-low credit allocated to micro, small and medium enterprises (MSMEs) are among the reasons behind Indonesia's low credit/GDP ratio. One of the most pressing consequences of it is the loss of invaluable opportunities, particularly the underutilization of potential for fostering businesses and other activities that could generate welfare growth and development progress in many lagging regions across the country.

To the extent credit allocation is closely related to money supply, and hence monetary policy, our analysis challenges the notion that because interregional inequality and monetary policy occupy distinct domains, where each is governed by its own dynamics and principles, they are not connected. We contend otherwise, substantiating our argument through a dual approach: quantitatively, by employing a robust model to provide empirical evidence in Chap. 5, and qualitatively, through insights gathered from questionnaire-based and interview-based surveys in Chap. 6.

After discussing the evidence of Indonesia's interregional inequality and its causes and repercussions in Chaps. 3 and 4, we investigate the association between monetary policy-driven money supply and interregional inequality in Chap. 5. The core aim is to challenge the perception that this association arises by chance, thereby reinforcing the validity and strength of the conceptual framework presented in Chap. 2.

Chapter 2
Space and Money

The importance of regional development for national growth is widely known. Although GDP is essentially the sum of all subnational (regional) GDP, synergy and interdependence between regions and between central and local economies play a critical role in the process. Given the interdependence among regions, individual regions could grow higher than they would individually, e.g., through sharing resources and ideas. When several regions work together, combining their development will achieve a greater national output compared to the case if they work alone. If they prosper and share resources and ideas with other regions, they can create a powerful interconnected network. This network is stronger in a system of subnational regions than in an international context and could fuel national advancement in ways that isolated growth could not. When subnational regions operate in synergy and embrace their interdependence, their seamless coordination fits together like puzzle pieces, painting a brighter picture of the overall economy.

The local-national relationship is symbiotic. Prospering regions foster national growth through resilience, competitiveness, and social stability, by way of, respectively, sectoral diversity, local innovation, and balanced growth. Vice versa, strong national growth supports its regions through infrastructure development, job creation, population distribution, and revenue generation. This symbiotic relationship applies to a set of development measures beyond growth. Non-growth-oriented national policies can also be made more effective as they receive support from regional development, e.g., policies for sustainable practices by using local resources and green technologies.

All these benefits are not merely to be appreciated; they need to be cultivated, as they are not preordained. The relationship between the center and the local government can ironically be detrimental to regional development. When natural resource-related activities in resource-rich regions are under the control of the center or other outside entities, they could worsen the welfare of the region. The benefits (sales, profits, export revenues) tend to be unequal, disproportionately accrued to

I. J. Azis, *Monetary Whispers Across Space*,
https://doi.org/10.1007/978-981-95-4625-1_2

those who control and manage the activities, and the burden falls exclusively on the region (social costs, environmental damage, resource depletion).

However, if a symbiotic relationship prevails, it has important implications. What is done at the national level could have significant impacts on development in subnational regions and, in turn, will shape the aggregate national outcome. To the extent that feedback effects between regional and national performance can play a crucial role in the overall outcome, both national and local policies matter for development. One of such roles is to influence the effectiveness of the policy. In the current study, our interest is particularly in assessing the effectiveness of national monetary policy.

Before delving into the subject, we will first revisit the concepts of and the interactions between regional and national development from the spatial economics perspectives. Due to the fundamental differences in the assumptions, specifications, and implications between spatial and non-spatial economics, we discuss those differences first.

2.1 Regional and National Development

When each region of a country is thriving, the whole nation becomes stronger and more resilient. Vice versa, when regions are shrinking. However, the mechanism is complex. It is more than just a simple arithmetic of adding outputs of all regions. More importantly, the intricate relationship involved in the mechanism can produce some unintended results. In this study, the unintended results we focus on are the growing interregional inequality. Two factors play a critical role in the mechanism: agglomeration forces and institutionally driven interactions between regions, including the role of social capital. Within the agglomeration concept, transport costs play a crucial role. To the extent incorporating transport costs in the analysis requires a different approach from that used in conventional economics, we will address this issue by first highlighting the distinction between conventional and spatial economics before discussing how transport costs shape interregional inequality.

2.1.1 Conventional Versus Spatial Economics

Lösch (1940) was among the first who emphasized the importance of space in economic analysis. In "The Economics of Location" (translated into English in 1954), he argued: "If everything occurred at the same time, there would be no development. If everything existed in the same place, there could be no particularity. Only space makes possible the particular, which then unfolds in time."The importance of space in economic analysis was depicted in his triangle relationship below, where the line between Production and Location captures the production of a location and

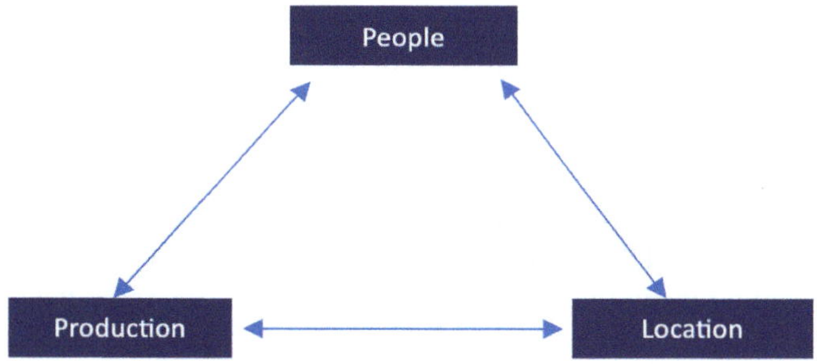

Fig. 2.1 Interrelationships between people, place and production. *Source*: Author's redrawing based on Lösch (1954)

the location of a production, the line between Production and People captures the production of people and the people of production, and the line between People and Location captures the location of people and the people of a location (Fig. 2.1).

In discussing the theme of a combination of man, work, and place, he explained the problem of occupational and spatial division of labor. Referring to the figure, the issues of interest were classified into six components (two for each arrow).

1. The problem of choice of an occupation was highlighted, where he emphasized the standard principle of comparative cost (commonly used in trade theory).
2. The problem of cooperation of men in an enterprise, where members of any given occupation have only one thing in common, i.e., to find their highest satisfaction in it where the principle of comparative cost also applies, although at the end it is not necessarily the most skillful in any ordinary sense who gather together in an occupation.
3. The problem of selecting a place to live or work that would affect the distribution of populations, for which the general principle is to select it so that nowhere else does he/she feel enough better to make up for the cost of moving, and the resulting real wages may be different from place to place due to transport costs.
4. The problems of urban sociology or the question of who occupies any given locality. For pure consumers, it amounts to finding the best residence, and for producers, it is to find the best combination of business place and residence. The locational distribution of activities can be determined by rent (land price), i.e., who is prepared to pay most (rent bidding).
5. The problem of developmental possibilities of a location, the applications of which could be limited by the fact that the theory tends to treat countries or regions as points, such that the locational configuration may not show the economic uniformity postulated by the principle of comparative cost.
6. The traditional location problem, where activities locate in where they yield the greatest profit with some degree of monopolistic elements, or, in the case of perfect competition, where they can continue to exist with a normal return on capital.

To the extent that people 'make' places and the fact that economic structures, employment opportunities, knowledge networks, educational and other public and social institutions exist in places, it can be deduced that places also 'shape' people. The emerging process would be the passing on of skills, learning, and spillovers of knowledge among workers in a local labor market (Martin, 2015). This process characterizes the phenomena of spatial agglomeration. Whether the labor market is high-skill or low-skill dominant, there will always be spillovers, and the prevailing institutional and cultural forms can reinforce them. This itself could already produce a widening gap between locations or regions. Thus, complex interrelationships between 'places' and people are an important source of any uneven spatial development.

Losch's view is in contrast to the dominant thinking of conventional and spaceless economics at that time. Unlike science, which is more of spirit, reason, and rationality, economics was seen to be related to the'material' because it was concerned with bread and butter matters (Azis, 2022). . Realizing that to understand better and to be realistic it is necessary to include'space' in economic analysis, Arrow and Debreu (1954) made an attempt to integrate'space' into economics. They defined the commodity not only by its physical characteristics but also by the place where it is made available. But two necessary implications make their analysis on a rocky ground: first, the same good traded in different places is treated as different economic commodities, which clearly violates the Law of One Price, where the same good available in different places should not be supplied at different prices; second, 'space' is not explicitly treated as location choices in the production and consumption specifications, so that the general equilibrium outcome of interdependence between markets cannot be guaranteed.

2.1.2 Transport Costs and Economies of Scale

It was Isard (1949, 1954, 1956) who criticized the Arrow-Debreu thesis and offered a different analysis based on modern location theory. By emphasizing the importance of'space' in economics and highlighting transport costs as the missing part of conventional economics, he persuasively argued that the inclusion of such costs warrants different methods of analysis, not just simply adding superscripts or subscripts to denote different regions in variables of interest (Isard, 1960, 1975, 1998). The relevant questions to ask in spatial economics are more than how much to produce, at what price, and at what combination of inputs given respective input prices. The relevant ones should also include where to locate the activity. With the inclusion of the'space' question, the optimal solution can be different from the standard equilibrium of a system that ignores location (as in conventional microeconomics). In fact, location is generally not of interest to conventional economists. The location is assumed to be given. In the words of Isard (1956): "production theory ... cannot justifiably treat certain production costs explicitly and other important ones implicitly in order to avoid the obstacles to analysis which the latter present." Obviously, when space (transport cost) enters the system, the solution of a standard optimization may not be the same.

It turns out that the implication of incorporating transport costs is more far-reaching than originally thought. It has significant consequences on both the theoretical part, particularly concerning the concept of equilibrium, and the policy implications, especially issues related to regional development and inequality.

From the theoretical part, when transport costs are treated explicitly, the spatial configuration and inequality can be very different from what standard neo-classical analysis suggests. Driven by market access (related to transport cost), local businesses and workers prefer to work in locations at which the total costs including transport costs are lower. Typically, these locations are in more developed regions close to the market where people tend to congregate, have greater purchasing power, and have better infrastructure. They may also prefer to locate near each other to gain benefits from external economies. Not only that they will have a larger pool of labor to choose from and pay lower input costs from joint purchases, but they can also share best practices, knowledge, and experiences. Ideas can flourish better and opportunities are also wider in a concentrated location such as an urban area (Romer, 1990). Workers with certain skills may find it more likely to find employment within clusters. However, if the trend occurs in an economy that is already characterized by a large gap between developed and less-developed regions, there is a risk that forces to concentrate will be further reinforced, resulting in a 'catastrophic agglomeration' with all its negative repercussions (Azis, 2020, 2022).

A noted theoretical implication of incorporating transport costs in the analysis is on the production-location equilibrium. The solution of a standard optimization in production theory can be very different from the optimum location solution. In a standard production theory, the main goal is to determine the most efficient way to allocate resources in order to maximize output or minimize costs. This is done by finding the optimal combination of inputs that will produce the desired level of output while minimizing the costs. One of the important concepts in such a model is the marginal rate of technical substitution (MRTS) and the elasticity of substitution (when percentage changes are used). They essentially describe the rate of change at which one input can be substituted for another to maintain the same level of output. Economies of scale is another important concept that describes how the cost per unit of output changes as the scale of production increases. Cases of decreasing, constant, and increasing returns to scale are identified based on such measures. All of these are useful concepts for helping companies make informed decisions about resource allocation and ways to improve overall efficiency and profitability.

What is missing is the role of transport costs. When these costs are included, the relevant additional question is: Where is the optimal location, and do firms find the optimal production first before the optimal location, or the reverse? There is therefore an element of sequence. As it turns out, only under a very strict condition, that is, when the firms' production function is homothetic, can the same production-location solution be obtained irrespective of the sequence. However, in reality, it is hard to find cases where the production function is homothetic. It is therefore unrealistic to think that it is not necessary to find the optimal location since it will be automatically determined. This is not much different than saying that location (or transport costs) is exogenous.

Another serious implication is on the stability of equilibrium. Consider two firms, A and B. Suppose α_s are revenues from activities that are not dependent on location, and p and q are prices and quantity, respectively. Firm A produces q_A and purchases q_B, while firm B produces q_B and purchases q_A. If the initial location of production of firm A is M and the location of B is N, and the rent cost to operate at these locations is rent_M and rent_N, their respective profits would be:

$$\pi_{AM} = \alpha_A + p_{AM}q_A - p_{BM}q_B - \text{rent}_M$$

$$\pi_{BN} = \alpha_B + p_{BN}q_B - p_{AN}q_A - \text{rent}_N$$

Consider a hypothetical case of reverse location, i.e., A is located in N instead of M, while B is in M instead of N. Since transport costs tc in spatial economics are not zero, the equilibrium price in such a hypothetical scenario would be:

$$p_{AN} = p_{AM} + tc_A > p_{AM}$$

$$p_{BM} = p_{BN} + tc_B > p_{BN}$$

That is, the price of the firm's product A and the firm's product B is equal to the price of A and B in their original locations plus the corresponding transport cost tc_A and tc_B. Their profits will depend on the rent at each location. Let us evaluate firm A, whose profit if it is located in N would be

$\pi_{AN} = \alpha_A + p_{AN}q_A - p_{BM}q_B - \text{rent}_N$

Comparing this with its profit if it is located in M (shown earlier) will give the following:

Suppose $\text{rent}_M \geq \text{rent}_N$. Substituting the expressions for transport costs into the above expression will give the following.

$\pi_{AN} - \pi_{AM} = (tc_A q_A + tc_B q_B + \text{rent}_M - \text{rent}_N) > 0$

That is, firm A will always have an incentive to move from M to N. Even if rent_M is not higher than rent_N, as long as the difference between the two is not substantial, there is still the possibility that firm A prefers to move from M to N because it will still make more profit by doing so. Therefore, when two locations have identical exogenous attributes, no feasible location pattern (equilibrium) can be sustained. None of the possible equilibria is stable because firms may move. This clearly defies one of the most fundamental conjectures in economics.

Graphically speaking, the key factor that leads to this 'surprising' conclusion is the non-convexity of the feasibility set caused by positive transport costs and the fact that firms have their respective location (specific address). Contrast this with the convexity assumption widely used in conventional economics. The simple 2-firm case in Fig. 2.2 below depicts the above formulation:

Holding other factors fixed, trade of good i between two locations, M and N, is equivalent to the standard case of transformation between two different goods since the availability of the same good at M and N gives rise to two different goods.

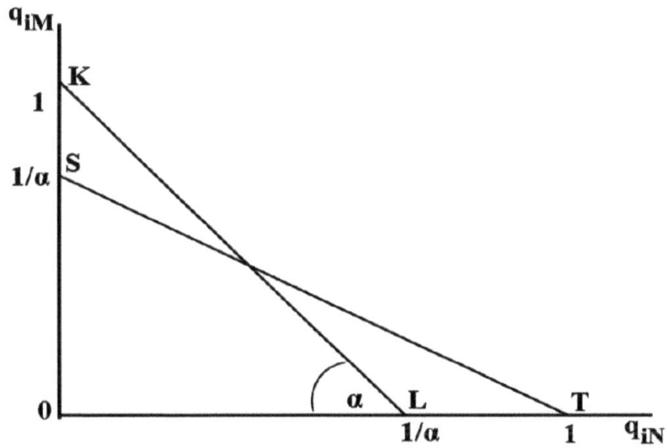

Fig. 2.2 Convexity in two-firm case. *Source*: Author's construction

It should be clear, therefore, that the existence and stability of the equilibrium in a standard general equilibrium theory hold only when the location is exogenous (given). If it is endogenous, where firms are free to choose their locations and the goods produced are indivisible, then the standard equilibrium in conventional economics can exist only in a "wonderland of no spatial dimensions."

There is also a fundamental implication on the general equilibrium framework of the analysis. The non-existence of competitive equilibrium described above leads to the following conjecture: in an economy with a finite number of locations, where space is homogeneous, transport is costly, and preferences are locally non-satiated, there exists no competitive equilibrium involving the transport of goods between locations. This is known as the 'Spatial Impossibility Theorem' (SIT).

When activities are perfectly divisible, the SIT implies that mobility of production factors is a perfect substitute for trade; that is, without any loss of efficiency, every activity occurs on a small scale in every possible place, as the transport costs are suppressed by producing exactly what they need where they are. But when activities are indivisible, even not perfectly, individual operations must take up space, complicating the set of interrelated activities, incurring transport costs. This essentially means that no competitive equilibrium is possible such that trade across space occurs, another defiance of the basic principles of economics. Thus, even though the consumption of individual input (say, land) is endogenous, the SIT remains valid because the positive trade costs and the fact that agents have an address in space make the feasible set nonconvex.

Clearly, freedom-to-move alters the basic tenets of the concept of competitive equilibrium in conventional economics. The most important implication for our analysis here is on the influence of all of the above on spatial configuration. What would be the consequence of the spatial economics concept on the outcome of spatial configuration, specifically on interregional inequality? Will the development process lead to convergence or divergence? Under what conditions is an outcome

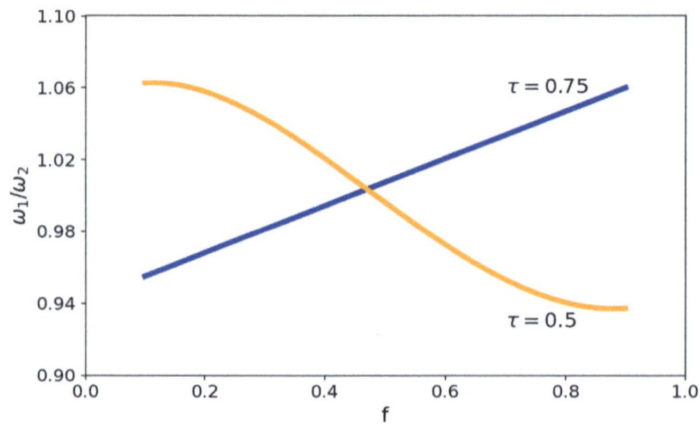

Fig. 2.3 Krugman's core-periphery model. *Notes*: τ indicates the fraction of delivered goods arrived at the destination; higher/lower τ indicates lower/higher transport costs. In Krugman (1991) $\tau = 0.75$ and $\tau = 0.5$ represent lower and higher transport cost, respectively. *Source*: Author's redrawing based on Krugman (1991)

more likely to occur than the other? How is it related to the concept of agglomeration, transport costs and economies of scale? These are important questions relevant to the analysis in this book.

Krugman (1991) elucidated the emergence of agglomeration through the phenomenon of geographical concentration of the manufacturing sector. Given certain specifications, his 'Core-Periphery' model shows that the interaction between transport costs and economies of scale will result in spatial concentration where the manufacturing sector tends to agglomerate in the core regions. Interestingly, the emergence of this pattern depends only on a few parameters. Considering the trade-off between the benefits of being close to a large market (core) and the costs of transporting goods to smaller and distant markets (periphery), he showed that lower transport costs can lead to concentration of manufacturing activities in the core region.

In a 2-dimensional graph of Fig. 2.3, where ω_1/ω_2 on the y axis denotes the wage ratio in region 1 and region 2, if the transport cost is low, reflected by a relatively high τ or the proportion of goods shipped to the destination, the relative real wage will increase when the share of workers in the manufacturing sector increases (change to the right in the x-axis). In such a scenario, a convergence process is taking place in which economies of scale and reduced transport costs drive workers to migrate to the core region.[1] This is the case where agglomeration forces are at play.

The process could also involve a feedback loop similar to Myrdal's concept of 'cumulative causation,' where the initial concentration force in the core attracts

[1] The divergence process, on the other hand, will occur when activities tend to disperse out of the core due to rising land price and labor costs.

more firms and workers, further improving the attractiveness and advantage of the core. Through these dynamics, more developed regions with better infrastructure will make better progress, causing the gap between developed and less developed regions to widen.

The policy implication of the core-periphery model is important: if reducing the gap between developed and less developed regions by increasing the production capacity and growth of less developed regions is to be achieved, government policies should focus on reducing transport costs and providing development incentives in those regions (place-based measures). In a broader context, reduced transport costs should be applied to cases within and between regions (e.g., between the core and the periphery), and the provision of development incentives is absolutely critical to ensure that local output and consumption in less developed regions will indeed increase. Why are these two policy implications important?

There is a widespread misconception about the role of infrastructure. Developing transport infrastructure does not necessarily lead to reduced transport costs. Depending on the type of infrastructure, it is highly possible that the newly built transport infrastructure makes transport costs more expensive. Consider the case of the construction of a new toll road. For low-income users, including small businesses who cannot afford to pay the toll, such infrastructure may result in higher, not lower, transport costs and hence gives no benefits to them. Instead, the new toll road may facilitate the inflows of goods from other regions, especially more developed ones, against which local products must compete. At the end of the day, the goods that local consumers need may be dominated by imported products rather than locally produced ones. If this happens with food products, the development costs would be even higher as local foods are generally healthier than imported ones, and the overreliance of basic necessities on imports makes local communities vulnerable.

The importance of providing incentives is also second to none. Without them, any additional spending in less developed regions could paradoxically worsen the interregional inequality. The Indonesian case discussed in Chap. 4 later shows how additional funds through bank credit in less developed regions outside Jawa and eastern Indonesia failed to stimulate the local economy due to a lack of production capacity and the incentives to boost it.

One may argue that as long as local activities can be facilitated by the new infrastructure, local output will increase and be further boosted by the multiplier effects. However, the validity of such an assertion depends on the type of goods and the nature of their use. If the new activities are related to natural resources (mining sector), the products of which are to be processed further elsewhere, not locally, the accrued value-added is very limited; so is the multiplier effect. However, the costs of final goods production elsewhere would be lower as a result of the increased supply of materials. As the final goods are produced in most cases in developed regions, the resulting outcome would be a growing gap between developed and less developed regions.

Cases may vary, but if the goal is to reduce interregional inequality by strengthening the production capacity of less developed regions, it is critical to select carefully

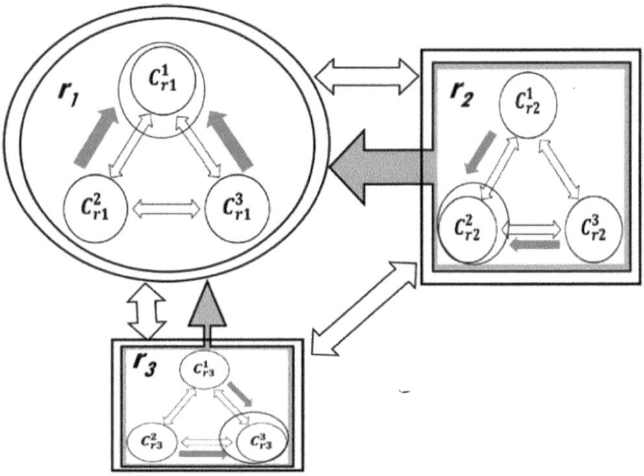

Fig. 2.4 Stylistic framework of development with agglomeration and intersectoral-interregional interactions. *Source*: Taken from Azis (2022)

what types of infrastructure and where to be built. Simply injecting more spending or building new infrastructure in less developed regions will not help reduce the gap. In some cases, it could even backfire by exacerbating the gap.

2.1.3 Stylized Framework

The following stylistic framework, taken from Azis (2022), epitomizes the development process characterized by the relationships between regions and the presence of agglomeration forces. Consider a case of three regions, r_1 -circle, r_2 -square, and r_3 -square, where the three sectors are represented by small circles in each region; for example, C_1r_1 denotes sector 1 in the region r_1 -circle, C_3r_3 denotes sectors 3 in the region r_3 -square, etc. (Fig. 2.4). The interactions between sectors and between regions are depicted in the Figure by clear arrows pointing towards two directions, and the agglomeration forces are represented by gray arrows pointing towards one direction. Let's assume that r_1-circle is the developed (core) region (has the largest area), and r_2-square and r_3-square are the less developed regions. The intraregional and interregional multipliers operating in the three activities in each region make all regions grow; this is represented by the expanded r_1 circle, r_2 square and r_3 square. However, external economies and agglomeration forces in the r_1-circle region also operate to increase regional growth. Hence, the external economies driven by agglomeration in C_1r_1, C_2r_2, and C_3r_3 (arrows in the one direction) cause an expansion in C_1r_1, C_2r_2, and C_3r_3, the precise size of which depends on the amount of external economies that can be absorbed by the sector. This is where the type and effectiveness of place-based incentives and policies matter.

Given the above specifications, all regions will expand, albeit at different rates, implying that the national economy grows. But we also see that the distribution between regions is altered, affecting the outcome of interregional inequality. The spatial inequality within each region is also altered by the intraregional agglomeration forces, e.g., capital city versus smaller cities, urban versus rural, etc. Hence, the final result displays national growth accompanied by a widening inequality between and within regions. Described in Chap. 3, this illustration exemplifies the case in Indonesia.

2.2 One Wheel, Many Roads

Regional development is a multidimensional concept that involves complex political, institutional, and cultural factors that shape regional and development policies. The spatial boundaries of it can be domestic (subnational regions) or international (groups of countries). It is a process through which human activities take place in some locations or regions to use the multifactor potentials or opportunities of the regions (Azis, 2020). Like national development, the goal is to achieve a better quality of life for all. However, what exactly the term "quality of life" means is not easy to define. Its assessment clearly depends on people's individual preferences that include things that matter most, for example, happiness, prosperity, personal capabilities, freedom of choice, self-esteem, respect, and dignity. However, measures to achieve this goal remain a subject of debate and contention.

The concept of regional development emerged from several intellectual traditions. The early thinking was heavily on economic issues. It began with neoclassical and regional growth theory, followed by Alfred Marshall's concept of external economies, and subsequently directed by David Ricardo towards trade theory through the concept of comparative advantage, where regions export intensive goods in resources they have abundantly. According to the concept, the initial endowment of a region matters and a particular pattern of interregional trade will emerge, known as interindustry trade. The subsequent concept of Krugman's New Economic Geography (NEG) highlighted the effect of a self-reinforcing agglomeration process by keeping monopolistic competition as the checkerboard, in which trade and incomes are not necessarily generated by differences in endowment but are accelerated through economies of scale, variety of goods, and skill composition. The emerging trade pattern under NEG is known as intra-industry trade (Krugman, 1991, 1995, 1996; Ottaviano & Puga, 1998).

With the features described above, the process of regional development can cause activities and people to concentrate in only selected areas (clusters), shaping the geographical diversity and unevenness in terms of economic, social, cultural, political, and environmental concerns. As a result, some regions may be more developed than others, creating inequality, which government intervention is expected to mitigate. This is the reason why regional development is sometimes also seen as the act or process of government providing funds and assistance to less developed regions.

2.2.1 Interregional Inequality Matters

From evolutionary thinking, interregional inequality was first viewed as a byproduct of national growth. This is similar to the case of inequality between income groups within a country. It is generally hypothesized that at a low level of income, inequality tends to worsen as income grows. After reaching a certain level of income, inequality will start to decline as income continues to grow. However, when it comes to evidence, such a U-shaped trend (Kuznets curve) does not always hold. Similarly, with the case of interregional inequality, where the evidence in opposition to the U-shaped hypothesis is found more frequently than in the case of inequality between income groups.

A more intriguing question is on the reverse causality, that is, the effect of inequality on growth and development. To what extent inequality between subnational regions affects national growth and what is the working mechanism. Several channels have been proposed, ranging from its effects through instability in economic institutions (market imperfections, lack of property right, rent seeking), social conditions (rising tension, social unrest, diminished trust), and political affairs (absence of check-and-balance, unequal rights, polarization), and unrealized potentials for higher growth and development due to unutilized capacity of some regions. When not all regions have equal access, members of society cannot reach their full potential. In addition to violating the rights of those members and defying the principles of equity and fairness, such conditions hinder the economy from being efficient and unable to maximize growth because not all resources and talents across regions are utilized.

Inequality could also prevent certain segments of the economy, such as income groups, social classes, or regions, from having equal access to health, education, and other basic services needed to improve their quality of life. When factor of production is mobile and no countervailing measures are in place, the initial inequality can create spiraling effects through migration and urbanization, potentially resulting in catastrophic agglomeration. Similarly, when only certain groups of society or regions are able to utilize factors of production, the system could fall into a virtuous cycle of growth, exacerbating the initial inequality.

For these reasons alone, addressing interregional inequality to promote inclusive growth is imperative. If inequality persists, different approaches and policies may be needed. Past policies may be obsolete, and their effectiveness becomes questionable. In some cases, place-based policies are warranted and need to be tailored to local conditions because certain place-based policies work only for specific locations. Even policies to promote balanced growth across different regions are likely to fail if the fundamental sources of interregional inequality are not addressed. Investment spending for infrastructure, education, and healthcare in less developed regions will not be effective if it is done without considering local institutions and dominant social capital. A similar faith could happen with a strategy of giving greater autonomy to local governments (decentralization).

The analysis in this book argues that addressing interregional inequality is important not only for the reasons described above, but also to make other policies, particularly monetary policy, more effective. Although seemingly unrelated, the aim of the book is to demonstrate the underlying connection between interregional inequality and monetary policy by uncovering the subtle, yet significant ways in which they intersect and influence one another. To have a better understanding of the matter, we will first dive into the role of money as the primary target of monetary policy in an economy.

2.2.2 Neutrality of Money

In a standard paradigm, microeconomics focuses on 'real' variables. The equilibrium construct is derived from an optimizing behavior given the preference system, production relations, and endowments, from which output, allocation, and relative prices are determined. The role of money and financial interrelations are virtually non-existent. Only 'real' factors and variables matter. In macro context, the stock of money only affects prices, exchange rates, and wages, not'real' variables such as GDP, investment, consumption, etc. Hence, money is neutral. Obviously, little can be used to guide the economy and policies from such a paradigm.

Even under the 'New Keynesian' models that became widely referred to since the 1980s, the concept of neutrality of money remained popular. The term 'money' itself has largely disappeared from discussions of monetary policy. The frequency of money in annual reports of major central banks declined over time (Von Hagen, 2004).[2] The central banks' shift towards controlling short-term interest rates, including within the framework of inflation targeting, rather than managing the money supply clearly had some influence on the trend. Perhaps this was partly due to the development of new financial instruments and technologies in which electronic payments and digital currencies have changed the way money is measured.

Not until Minsky (1993) made an argument about money being an active force to influence economic stability, was a new thinking established. In Minsky's view, the role of money in the economy is dynamic and intertwined, in which state policies, along with the behavior of banks, financial institutions, and financial markets, play a crucial role in improving financial stability and the economy. But they can also create financial turmoil and a crisis. As market incentives drive banks to the creation of assets, they increase their size to compete for capital with non-financial institutions through all kinds of innovation. In the process, increased risk taking through excessive borrowing and speculative behavior emerges, and that could result in a build-up of debt and financial fragility. When debt levels become unsustainable,

[2] Former Governor of the Bank of England also noticed that there is a paradox in the role of money in economic policy. On the one hand, price stability has become the central objective of central banks, but central banks' attention to money has been declining (King, 2002).

the system becomes vulnerable to financial instability and economic downturns. This is the reason why, in his "financial instability hypothesis", Minsky argued forcefully that government, as both policy makers and regulators, should play a significant role in ensuring that such behaviors are prevented by regulating the operations of the financial market. His articulation about financial regulation and supervision becomes the basis of a framework for what is later known as 'macro-prudential regulation. Unlike microprudential measures, where the idiosyncratic features of individual financial institutions are the central target of evaluation (to avoid bank runs and defaults at particular institutions), macroprudential policies address interactions between individual institutions and the financial system as a whole. The evaluation is based on cash flow, where bank liquidity is evaluated not as an innate feature of a particular class of assets; instead it is influenced by the balance sheet of the institutions, the markets (for those assets), the financial system, and the economic condition as a whole. Consequently, failures in one financial institution will have repercussions on other institutions, potentially disrupting the entire financial markets and the economy.

At any rate, one fundamental conclusion of Minsky's analysis is that money is not neutral. In addition to being a medium of exchange, money affects the economy in crucial ways through financing activities such as investment and consumption. The behaviors of investors and consumers, that is, how businesses and individuals plan and invest and how consumers spend and save, are influenced by the availability and value of money. In times of economic uncertainty, people may save more and spend less, affecting overall economic activity. When the economy is in crisis, investors have low confidence and lose their appetite to expand.

This is where the role of banks as credit allocators becomes critical. As banks and other financial institutions allocate credit and extend loans, they create money and add money supply that, in turn, will influence economic activity. Through this mechanism, monetary policy and the behavior of banks could have important impacts on the economy. The effectiveness of the policy in achieving the intended goals is an important issue that we will explore next.

2.2.3 Policy's Channel of Transmission

Initially, 'monetary policy' was defined as the actions of the central bank to influence some measures of money stock (money supply or high power money). As more and more central banks used nominal interest rates as a target, the interpretation of 'monetary policy' was transformed. Some central banks also began to target the nominal exchange rate.

Attempting to evaluate the effectiveness of monetary policy by comparing certain monetary targets with actual achievements seems to make sense. But as 'rational expectation' theory (Ratex) became popular in the 1980s, the idea of targeting money stocks, interest rates, or exchange rates was seriously questioned. One of the issues was the lack of a "nominal anchor". According to Ratex, if central banks set targets for nominal interest rates, any nominal variables, including the price level, would be indeterminate. Taylor (1993) suggested that a desired or target inflation rate could be used as the 'nominal anchor'. This led to the famous Taylor rule in monetary policy that continues to be adopted by many central banks until today.

Under Ratex, it is assumed that people will anticipate any central bank policy (whether targeting money supply, interest rates, or exchange rate) and incorporate it into their expectations, before adjusting their behavior accordingly in ways that can neutralize the impact of the policy. For example, if the market expects the central bank to raise interest rates, people might anticipate lower inflation and adjust wages and prices accordingly. That could lead to an increase in demand. Higher demand could, in turn, neutralize the intended tightening effect of the policy on output. Vice versa, if the market expects that central bank will raise money supply to stimulate the economy, people will adjust or raise wages and prices because they anticipate higher inflation, in such a way that an expansionary monetary policy likely fails to achieve its stimulative role.

This is the reason why, according to Ratex, only unexpected, unpredictable, and credible policy can have real effects on the economy.[3] If a monetary policy is already expected, it will not be effective as it will fail to influence the real economy. Even if the policy is unexpected, but the market questions the credibility and commitment of the central bank, people's expectations will not necessarily align with the policy, making it more difficult to achieve the policy goals. This so-called "policy ineffectiveness proposition" became popular in New Classical Macroeconomics (Sargent & Wallace, 1975). Essentially, it implies that it is not relevant to discuss the effectiveness of monetary policy.

One of the key determinants for this conclusion was the assumption of perfectly flexible wages and/or prices (Taylor, 1980; Calvo, 1983). Intuitively, it is not difficult to trace the mechanism in which, when allowed by the flexibility assumption, any perturbation (i.e., a change in monetary policy) will cause some adjustments and will eventually revert the system back to an equilibrium similar to the initial one. That is, any changes in real variables caused by a monetary policy shock would be temporary, confirming the ineffectiveness of monetary policy. However, achieving perfect flexibility is far from reality. It is unattainable, elusive, and unrealistic. Absent of it, most adjustments would not bring real variables back to the pre-policy levels. Monetary policy will therefore have some impacts on both the nominal and real variables.

[3] On the impact of monetary policy on real sector, Ratex and the New Keynesian (emerged in the 1970s–1980s as a response to Ratex criticisms of traditional Keynesian economics) offer different perspectives: monetary policy has limited to no effect on real economic variables according to Ratex (mainly due to market already anticipated the policy), while the New Keynesian argued that monetary policy can have significant effects on real economic variables due to slow adjustments of price and wage (sticky). From the perspective of monetary policy effectiveness, the New Keynesian advocated for clear and consistent monetary policy rules, such as the Taylor Rule, to make monetary policy more effective in achieving economic stability.

Another unrealistic assumption, yet, which is very fundamental in Ratex, is that people are forward-looking, able to form expectations about the future based on their understanding of economic policy and available information. Obviously, this is another conjecture that is far from realistic, let alone in countries where the quality of information and the ability of people to comprehend economic policy to form expectations are limited.

In reality, policy is hardly neutral. Even the nationally-determined monetary policy could have significant and diverse impacts on the economy of different subnational regions. Some of those impacts may correspond to the policy goals (effective); some may not be in line with what the policy aims at (ineffective). It is therefore imperative to evaluate the effectiveness of monetary policy, including its diverse impacts on subnational regions.

There are several channels through which monetary policy affects the real economy. The traditional channel is the interest rate channel, where changes in the cost of borrowing directly reflected in the interest rates determined by the central bank will affect the output and aggregate demand components, such as investment and consumption. Another channel is the bank lending channel, where monetary policy affect banks' (lenders') balance sheet in such that it determines their ability to lend. However, note that the bank's ability can be different from the bank's willingness to lend. The latter is influenced by more complex factors that reflect the behavior of the bank. One of the indicators commonly used to estimate behavior toward credit allocation is the loan-to-deposit ratio. Yet, while this ratio is frequently cited as an indicator of bank behavior, it may present a distorted view, as it fails to capture the nuances of daily banking operations. A more insightful method for understanding how banks allocate credit is to engage directly with banking practitioners through targeted discussion and observation (more on this in Chap. 6).

Next, we have the balance sheet channel, where the financial structure of the borrowers is affected by monetary policy. The net worth of investors and the collateral values reflected in their balance sheet can be improved or worsened by monetary policy. When improved, they borrow and spend. When things worsen, they stop spending. The final outcome is therefore influenced by their actions.

Another mechanism can work through the exchange rate channel. Weakening currency triggered by lower interest rates can boost exports and make imports more expensive. The opposite effect applies when the central bank raises the interest rates. At the regional level, the mechanism works indirectly, because there is only one national exchange rate, the magnitude of which cannot be controlled or managed by local banks or any regional institutions.

Monetary policy can also affect the real economy through the wealth effect channel, in which the transmission operates through changes in prices of financial and non-financial assets that reflect the wealth of asset holders. The level of wealth can, in turn, affect businesses and households' decisions whether to invest/spend or not. They may also compare the market value of their assets with replacement costs. If, for example, the interest rates are lowered, the market value of the assets may go up so that it becomes higher than the replacement costs. In such circumstances, businesses can increase their investment and replace existing capital equipment with new ones. However, in less developed countries this channel (also known as Tobin's q channel) is not too relevant, as the size and influence of wealth on the real sector are limited. Even if the influence is substantial, it occurs only in a few regions within the country.

Another important channel, yet not easy to quantify, is the expectation channel. In particular, when the public and the market believe that the central bank is going to honor its commitment, say to keep the interest rates low, businesses and consumers will make decisions based on the premise that future growth of the economy will be higher. This may stimulate investment and spending, boosting the real economy.

The last is the credit channel. This channel is highly relevant when applied to the analysis of monetary policy effect on the real economy at subnational regional levels. It encompasses not only the bank lending channel described earlier, but also the balance sheet channel, involving the supply of credit and the demand for borrowing. The primary indicator to use is the difference in the cost of internal and external financing. In the credit channel, the transmission works from monetary policy to borrowers' balance sheets that would affect the cost of obtaining credit, and lenders' balance sheets that would affect the availability of credit. If, for example, the central bank decides to increase the interest rates, this would raise the external finance premium, making external financing more expensive relative to internal financing. The financial structures of the borrowers tend to deteriorate and this will reduce their ability to borrow. Reduced capacity will reduce the demand for credit, investment, and spending. Hence, unlike the bank lending channel that places emphasis on the role of banks in credit supply, the credit channel examines both the cost of loans viewed from the borrowers' balance sheet condition and the availability of credit viewed from the lenders' balance sheet position.

Depending on the transmission channels, regional responses to monetary policy are different between regions. The evaluation of those responses must consider the different conditions and characteristics of different regions. The choice of impacted variables also matters (Beare, 1976). In the case where regional prices are the indicator of impact, the intensity of monetary policy transmission could be different from region to region. If regional output is the variable of interest, where bank credit plays an important role, different degrees of liquidity preference between banks in regions will produce heterogeneous impacts.

At a more micro-level, the conditions and characteristics of different regions are reflected in the behavior of firms in each region. If a large share of firms in a region have tighter financial constraints (e.g., limited by tighter borrowing constraints), even under expansionary monetary policy, they will likely reduce their investment, making the policy less effective. One of the reasons for such behavior is the fact that constrained firms tend to bear greater costs from making wrong decisions when there is a change in economic conditions. Hence, they respond more quickly and adjust their prices faster than what unconstrained firms will do, although their information processing capacities may be limited. Some label this behavior as having greater attentiveness to monetary policy changes (Rezghi, 2025). To the extent firm size is commonly used as a proxy for financial constraints (Gertler & Gilchrist, 1994), this hypothesis implies that in a country where the number of micro, small and medium enterprises (MSME) is high, the effectiveness of monetary policy is likely lower.

Implicit in the above analysis is the presence of 'financial frictions' that can influence the effectiveness of monetary policy through the investment channel. According to Gertler and Gilchrist (1994) and Bernanke et al. (1999) the net worth of the firm determines the external finance premium through a mechanism called 'financial accelerator'. The arising premium will amplify the real effects of monetary policy. By assuming that borrowers have full information about monetary shocks, Ottonello and Winberry (2018) highlighted the role of financial frictions by arguing that they can force financially constrained firms to be less responsive to monetary shocks.

Some of the impacts of monetary policy can also be the result of spillovers from other regions affected by the policy, as well. Even if only a particular sector is affected, the effect on other regions could be across sectors. If a monetary policy directly affects the retail trade sector in one region, the spillover effects in other regions may be felt in sectors beyond just retail trade. If the services sector is the most affected in one region, the manufacturing sector in other regions could be the one that receives the biggest spillovers. Housing is another sector often impacted by changes in monetary policy. Regional differences in the housing market will generate heterogeneous responses to housing prices, mortgage rates, and housing investment in different regions. In turn, this will generate different responses in terms of household consumption (Garriga et al., 2017). In some cases, the spillover effects can be transmitted to surrounding regions through feedbacks from adjacent markets.[4]

Whatever the nature and intensity of the regional impacts of monetary policy, they change over time (Owyang & Wall, 2009). Hence, any analysis on the subject should ideally employ a specific model that takes into account the dynamic changes in the relationships among variables. An example is the vector autoregressive (VAR) models. Using data from US regions, Dominguez-Torres and Hierro (2019) reviewed this topic using VAR and the federal fund rate as the policy indicator. They found that there were indeed heterogeneous responses across regions to Fed policy.

2.2.4 *Effectiveness of Policy and Heterogenous Impacts*

Measuring the effectiveness of monetary policy is always challenging. There are too many dimensions and types of uncertainty within which central banks operate. This makes it difficult to gauge the effectiveness of the policy within a certain time frame.

The logical way to measure it is by comparing targets and achievements. For example, one can compare the explicit numeric inflation target and the observed rates of inflation. Using moving averages of both indicators, Rasche and Williams (2005) tried to determine the maximum period for which the inflation rate remains

[4] Ignoring spatial interactions may result in bias estimations Brady (2011, 2014).

within the bounds determined by the inflation target. Applying it to 21 countries that had announced explicit numeric inflation targets, they were able to identify countries in which monetary policy has been very effective and countries where the observed inflation rates have consistently missed their target ranges; some missed the target on the high side, others on the low side.

However, it is difficult to pinpoint the main reasons behind the gap between the target and the annual numbers. It cannot be only due to policy ineffectiveness, as other factors have some roles as well. Delays in policy transmission are one of them. It takes time for any monetary policy to have a meaningful effect on inflation. Another important factor is expectation, which can be influenced by news, policy announcements, and the credibility of the central bank. Supply-side shock (e.g., global commodity prices, supply chain disruptions, weather) could also cause the actual inflation to deviate from the targets.[5]

Considering the fact that today central banks have multiple objectives, e.g. price stability, close to full employment, stable exchange rate, and financial stability, gauging the effectiveness of monetary policy is very challenging. Exogenous events (domestic, regional and global) and other policies (e.g. fiscal) may also complicate the evaluation, since it is not easy to isolate their effects from those caused by changes in monetary policy.[6] Another factor that could affect the evaluation results is the presence of lagged effects. It may take several months, or even years, for changes in interest rates or other monetary policy measures to fully impact the economy. The way monetary policy affects the economy can vary over time depending on factors such as new banking regulation and the usage of financial instruments, including digital money.

In terms of impact on different subnational regions, monetary policy clearly affects the economy differently across regions. Economic agents in different regions may also have different expectations about economic conditions and future policies in such a way that the saving and spending adjustments they make may differ across regions. All of the above, including constraints on data (the availability and quality), could limit our ability to evaluate the effectiveness of monetary policy accurately.

What does the effectiveness of monetary policy have to do with regional development? More specifically, what role does it play in addressing interregional inequality? Can inequality between regions alter the effectiveness of monetary

[5] Another possible reason for monetary policy to be ineffective is the super low or near zero nominal interest rates. This occurred in Japan for more than a decade and in the United States during the 2008 global financial crisis, forcing the authority to take alternative tools such as quantitative easing (QE).

[6] The role of fiscal policy in affecting the effectiveness of monetary policy is widely known. But one of the most debated issues around that subject is the case of 'tight money paradox' raised by Sargent and Wallace (1981) and Leeper (1991), who argued that higher interest rates could paradoxically cause inflation expectations to go up if there is no response from fiscal policy (in particular, a response to the primary balance). When real interest rates are raised, debt levels go up, and the market expects there will be monetization, reducing the effectiveness of the policy (becoming counterproductive). Hence, the behavior of fiscal policy is key to the effectiveness of monetary policy.

policy? At subnational level, the conduct and behavior of local banks have profound repercussions on money supply and hence regional economy. Since money is not a static entity, but a dynamic force capable of influencing economic cycles, the conduct of local banks with respect to credit allocation has a direct influence on local money supply. It is through this mechanism that local banks can affect regional liquidity. Their decision and behavior on credit availability, interest rates, and borrowing rules could play a significant role in regional development.

When the role of local banks is juxtaposed with the agglomeration-driven inequality, a clearer link is established between regional development and the effectiveness of monetary policy. The bulk of the discussions in Chap. 5 are based on this ground. As local banks' credit is the predominant money supply at the regional level and that money supply is the crucial tool of the central bank in the conduct of monetary policy, the effectiveness of the latter can be directly influenced by what and how local banks allocate credit.

Of course, there are other factors that influence the effectiveness of monetary policy. It is well known that factors ranging from the overall state of the economy, the health of banking and financial systems, the political condition manifested in fiscal policy, and the trust and confidence of the market over the central bank and the broader economy will all have some influence on the effects of monetary policy. Another important factor is financial innovation and the rapid advancement in financial technology. Given the speed of advancement, the monetary authority will find it more difficult to control the process of money creation. The adoption of digital currencies, for example, can raise the probability that the outcome deviates from what is intended by the policy.

Then there is an external environment that could influence the effectiveness of the policy. An upturn (downturn) in the global economy can reinforce (limit) the impact of the authority's efforts to stimulate the national economy. This itself would have already impacted the subnational economy in a meaningful way. A downturn in global commodity prices would adversely affect commodity-dependent regions more than the rest of the country. Regions with a more developed financial market would receive greater negative spillovers from a global financial crisis through financial contagion compared to regions with a limited financial market.

If economic fluctuations due to monetary policy are evenly distributed across regions, no region would change (improve or worsen) its relative position with respect to the rest of the country. Any effects in the regions will be temporary, because in the long run these effects dissipate. This is equivalent to the 'money is neutral' proposition where regional growth would depend only on real factors. However, as discussed earlier, this concept is flawed. In a modern economy, money is not neutral and the effect of monetary policy is not evenly distributed across regions.

Regional differences in economic, social, and demographic structure, as well as in policies and level of development, could influence the extent and intensity of the impact. Regions having a large share of interest rate sensitive sectors will be impacted more by the change in the interest rates. The impact of rising interest rates in regions that are dominated by retail trade will be greater than in regions that are dominated by agriculture, because trade activities often rely on credit borrowing.

Similarly, the impact of the change in interest rates will be greater in regions where most businesses are small and medium (SME) types because small businesses often rely on bank borrowing. Local communities with a strong habit of spending, either due to cultural or demographic reasons (e.g., young age dominant) are more sensitive to changes in interest rates.

The policy response of the regional government also matters. To alleviate the impact of the high cost of money after an increase in interest rates, the local government can provide subsidies to local lenders through a local government-owned bank (such as Bank Pembangunan Daerah, BPD). Such a policy might be taken to prevent the local cost of borrowing from rising. More developed regions with higher levels of investment and better infrastructure tend to be more resilient to interest rates increase and more able to reap the benefits from a fall in interest rates. To the extent the level of local development is also reflected in the stage of local bank and financial sector development, the impact of a change in interest rates tends to be more muted in less developed regions than in developed regions because the latter have more developed financial markets and institutions. A loose monetary policy will provide more opportunities for borrowers to access credit and investment opportunities in developed regions.

In an archipelago like Indonesia, where some islands comprise several regions/provinces, the tightness of connections among regions can be a significant source of spatial spillover. Activities in one region can easily affect neighboring regions in such a way that the indirect impact of interest rate change in less developed regions can be significant, although the direct impact is muted (large only in other regions). Another channel that makes the effect of monetary policy different between regions works through changes in the exchange rate. Loose monetary policy can affect exporting regions positively and importing regions negatively through the depreciation of the exchange rate.

Nonetheless, at the end of the day, a more direct impact is influenced by the behavior of local banks and the structure of the local economy. Through a rather complex mechanism, these two factors can generate an unexpected outcome, different from what the monetary policy intends to achieve. The role of the bank's behavior in affecting regional development is derived from the premise that money is not only not neutral but also endogenous. This makes the behavioral approach different from the monetarist and Keynesian approach.

The conclusion that monetary policy will have different impact across regions is shared by both approaches. But monetarists and Keynesians are different in terms of transmission channels: one is through different business cycles due to regional differences in income or wealth elasticity of demand (the monetarists), and the other is through different regional responses to aggregate demand components such as consumption and investment, which react to monetary policy change (the Keynesians). In both cases, different regional responses reflect different sensitivity to business cycles and interest rate changes, all driven by a different economic structure, making them labeled as the 'structural approach'.

Both monetarist and Keynesian approaches treat money supply as exogenous. This is what makes the 'behavioral approach' different from both. In the 'behavioral approach', the money supply is endogenously influenced by the behavior of banks. To evaluate the effect of monetary policy under this approach, therefore, it is necessary to examine the factors that can affect the behavior of banks. And since lending transactions involve lenders and borrowers, this also means factors that affect the behavior of borrowers should be included.[7] One of such factors is the liquidity preference between the borrowers and the lenders.

Liquidity preference refers to how agents (lenders and borrowers) value cash relative to interest-bearing assets over varying lengths of time. From the lender's point of view, it represents the ability of lenders to meet cash demands (cash holdings, currency, or accounts in central banks), and from the borrowers' point of view, it represents their ability to easily find cash when needed. In our surveys of local banks throughout several regions, one of the indicators that lenders use as a reference is the liquidity coverage ratio (LCR), which is the ratio of liquid assets to total net cash over a given period. Some also use the ratio between current assets and current liabilities or simply the difference between the two.

In the context of analyzing the impact of monetary policy on regional development, the endogenous nature of money supply under the behavioral approach implies that the resulting regional distribution of credit is determined not by how to divide a given amount of credit among different regions but by exploring the question why given the interest rates in some regions banks lend more (inelastic supply) than in others (elastic supply); see Rodríguez-Fuentes (2006). In other words, if one region gets more credit, it does not necessarily mean other regions will get less. Any credit increase in a region is achieved by expanding the national money supply. In this sense, the regional money supply grows according to the region's need, from which the overall national money supply adjusts accordingly.

The amount of credit that local banks allocate will directly translate into the size of the money supply at the local level. But its repercussions on the local economy are uncertain because what local borrowers do with the credit matters crucially. The actual amount of money circulating in the region is influenced by what and where the borrowers spend the money, such that the interregional distribution of local credit may not reflect the distribution of economic activities between regions. Credit allocated in region r_3 in Fig. 2.4 may not be spent in that region. Through the forces of agglomeration and transport cost discussed earlier, many businesses may prefer to operate outside the region, choosing r_1 or r_2 despite the fact that the credit was received and recorded in region r_3. From our field studies, we found several cases in which financing of activities in a region originated from credit issued in another region.

A more often case is where the bulk of the credit fund is spent in other regions, although the activities remain in the same region where credit is extended. There is a disconnect between the location of the allocated credit and the region where the money is actually spent. This arrangement takes place very often in less-developed

[7] With the prominence of banks' behavior, financial regulation–not only monetary policy–also plays an important role in affecting the regional economy through bank credit. This makes it more difficult to assess the impact of monetary policy, let alone the effectiveness of it.

regions outside of Jawa and eastern Indonesia, where the structure of the economy is overwhelmingly trade dominant. The nature of trade business (i.e., purchase goods to be sold) is such that most of the money is spent to buy goods wherever they are available. If they are not available locally, the purchase is made elsewhere. In many less developed regions outside of Jawa and Eastern Indonesia, the proportion spent outside the regions can reach as high as 100% as the purchased goods are not available locally, either because the local economy does not have the capacity to produce them, or they have a lack of supporting infrastructure. This explains why in many poor regions we visited we found most credit issued by local banks was not spent locally by the borrowers. At the same time, this is another example that highlights the importance of two policy implications of Krugman's center-periphery model discussed above, ie, place-based incentives and reduced transport costs. It also demonstrates that regional credit allocation does not reflect the regional distribution of production activities.

It should be noted that most business enterprises rely on bank credit. Statistics shows that of the total credit issued by local banks the largest share goes to non-tradeable sector, especially trade services, mostly in the form of credit for working capital, and a large portion of it was spent outside the region. This asymmetry has serious implications for regional development and inequality. The multiplier effects of local credit are small, so any increase in credit in poor regions fails to reduce the development gap between these regions and the more developed ones. In some cases, the gap could be even wider because increased spending in developed regions further stimulates growth. Obviously, several factors influence the precise extent of the gap and its trend over time.

This brings to the fore the connection between interregional inequality and effectiveness of monetary policy, the central thesis of this book.

A monetary policy is said to be effective if it can achieve most of the intended objectives. The typical policy objectives are stable prices (low inflation and stable exchange rate) and full employment (associated with healthy growth of the economy). Given that spatial inequality is a natural consequence of the development process, monetary policy always operates in a system that has some degrees of interregional inequality, implying that the policy has different effects in different regions. Earlier, we listed a number of factors that led to different impacts of monetary policy across regions. Let us now delve into the link between interregional inequality and monetary policy.

Many studies have shown that the impact of monetary easing in regions with higher unemployment and lower flexibility of the labor market (typically less developed regions) is less pronounced than in regions with more dynamic labor markets. In general, developed regions can respond to monetary policy more positively and be able to capture greater benefits than less developed regions. The asymmetry also applies in the reverse case: adverse effects of monetary tightening tend to be longer-lasting in poor regions than in wealthier regions. The reason is because parts of the variables targeted by monetary policy are unequally distributed in a country with high interregional inequality. Poor and less developed regions have very limited financial markets and services, preventing them from offering greater access to financial resources (credits and other financial assets). Any favorable impact intended by monetary policy will have only limited effectiveness. Lower interest rates and asset prices may not mean much in an economy where access to credit is limited and financial assets are nonexistent.

This indicates that the transmission of monetary policy depends on the inequality between regions. In a high interregional inequality condition, the channels of monetary policy work less uniformly across regions, and the overall response to the policy is less synchronized. In such a condition, the intended changes of aggregate variables (GDP growth, inflation, unemployment) cannot be consistently realized, reducing the effectiveness of the policy.

If the process continues, the risk of having a low effectiveness of the policy can be even higher. The example of bank credit largely going to the trade sector cited earlier exemplifies the possibility that the initial inequality between regions can get worse if credit in less developed regions is largely spent outside the regions due to a lack of local supply. In Fig. 2.5, this is depicted by the bottom arrow pointing rightward from the 'Monetary Policy: Credit' box to 'Output: Regional-National' box and the bottom arrow pointing leftward from that box toward 'Spatial Inequality.' The more bank credit is allocated, the larger the development gap. On the one hand, increased spending will stimulate growth and greater multipliers in developed regions, on the other hand, less developed regions remain stagnant, unable to break the downward cycle. This causes a simultaneous occurrence of a virtuous cycle of growth in developed regions and a vicious cycle of decline in the rest of the country, exacerbating both the interregional inequality and the ineffectiveness of monetary policy.

To break the cycle, addressing inequality between regions should be a part of the considerations in formulating monetary policy. Given the prevailing gap between developed and less developed regions, monetary policy could inadvertently

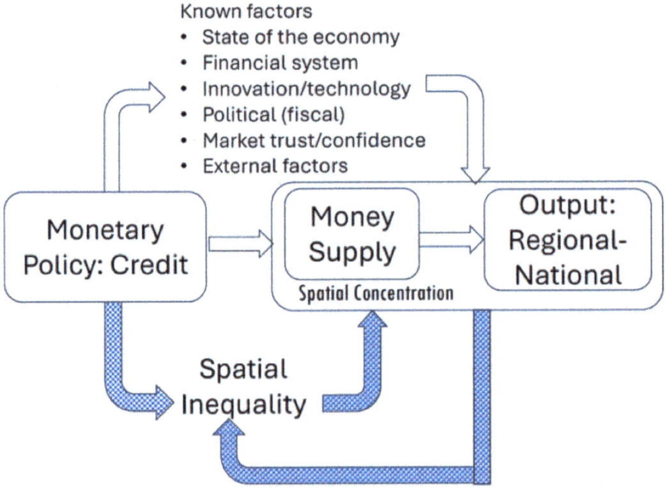

Fig. 2.5 Spatial inequality and effectiveness of monetary policy. *Source*: Author's construction

exacerbate the gap and become less effective in stimulating nationwide growth. Even ignoring the dynamics of the process, the results could still deviate from the outcome intended by the policy. This is the reason why in some countries monetary authority began to pay more attention to how the role of inequality and heterogeneity plays in the transmission of monetary and other macro policies. There is clearly a growing recognition that the pass-through of monetary policy is dependent on heterogeneity factors (Yellen, 2016; Ahn et al., 2017).

References

Ahn, S., Kaplan, G., Moll, B., Winberry, T., & Wolf, C. (2017). When inequality matters for macro and macro matters for inequality. *NBER Macroeconomics Annual, 32*, 1–75.

Arrow, K. J., & Debreu, G. (1954). Existence of an equilibrium for a competitive economy. *Econometrica, 22*(3), 265–290.

Azis, I. J. (2020). Regional development and noneconomic factors. In A. Kobayashi (Ed.), *International encyclopedia of human geography* (2nd ed., Vol. 11, pp. 269–274). Elsevier. https://doi.org/10.1016/B978-0-08-102295-5.10117-9

Azis, I. J. (2022). *Periphery and small ones matter: Interplay of policy and social capital*. Springer.

Beare, J. (1976). A monetarist model of regional business cycles. *Journal of Regional Science, 16*, 57–63.

Bernanke, B. S., Gertler, M., & Gilchrist, S. (1999). The financial accelerator in a quantitative business cycle framework. In J. B. Taylor, & M. Woodford (Eds.), *Handbook of macroeconomics* (Vol. 1). North Holland.

Brady, R. R. (2011). Measuring the diffusion of housing prices across space and over time. *Journal of Applied Econometrics, 26*, 213–231.

Brady, R. R. (2014). The spatial diffusion of regional housing prices across U.S. States. *Regional Science and Urban Economics, 46*, 150–166.

Calvo, G. A. (1983). Staggered prices in a utility-maximizing framework. *Journal of Monetary Economics, 12*(3), 383–398.

Dominguez-Torres, H., & Hierro, L. A. (2019). The regional effects of monetary policy: A survey of the empirical literature. *Journal of Economic Surveys, 33*(2), 604–638.

Garriga, C., Kydland, F. E., & Šustek, R. (2017). Mortgages and monetary policy. *Review of Financial Studies, 30*(10), 3337–3375.

Gertler, M., & Gilchrist, S. (1994). Monetary policy, business cycles, and the behavior of small manufacturing firms. *Quarterly Journal of Economics, 109*(2), 309–340.

Isard, W. (1949). The general theory of location and space-economy. *The Quarterly Journal of Economics, 63*(4), 476–506.

Isard, W. (1954). Location theory and international and interregional trade theory. *The Quarterly Journal of Economics, 68*(1), 97–114.

Isard, W. (1956). *Location and space-economy, a general theory relating to industrial location, market areas, land use, trade, and urban structure*. New York: The Technology Press of M. I. T. and John Wiley and Sons, Inc.

Isard, W. (1960). *Methods of regional analysis: An to regional science*. The MIT Press.

Isard, W (1975). *Introduction to regional science*. Prentice-Hall.

Isard, W., Azis, I., Drennan, M., Miller, R., Saltzman, S., & Thorbecke, E. (1998). *Methods of interregional and regional analysis*. Routledge.

King, M. (2002). No money, no inflation: The role of money in the economy. *Bank of England Quarterly Bulletin, Summer*, 162–177.

Krugman, P. (1991). *Geography and trade*. MIT Press.

Krugman, P. (1995). *Development, geography, and economic theory*. MIT Press.

Krugman, P. (1996). *The self-organizing economy*. Blackwell.
Leeper, E. M. (1991)yEquilibria under 'active' and 'passive' monetary and fiscal policies. *Journal of Monetary Economics, 27*, 129–147.
Lösch, A. (1940). *Die röumliche Ordnung der Wirtschaft. Eine Untersuchung über Standort, Wirtschaftsgebiete und internationalen Handel*. Published by Jena, Gustav Fischer.
Lösch, A. (1954). *The economics of location*. Yale University Press.
Martin, R. (2015). Rebalancing the spatial economy: The challenge for regional theory. *Territory, politics, governance*, Routledge.
Minsky, H. P. (1993). On the non-neutrality of money. *Federal Reserve Bank of New York Quarterly Review, 18*(1), 77–82.
Ottaviano, G .I. P., & Puga, D. (1998). Agglomeration in the global economy: A survey of the 'new economic geography. *The World Economy, 21*, 707–731.
Ottonello, P., & Winberry, T. (2018). Financial heterogeneity and the investment channel of monetary policy. *NBER Working Paper*, No. 2422.
Owyang, M. T., & Wall, H. J. (2009). Regional VARs and the channels of monetary policy. *Applied Economics Letters, 16*, 1191–1194.
Rasche, R., & Williams, M. M. (2005). The effectiveness of monetary policy. *Working Paper No. 2005-048B*. Federal Reserve Bank of St. Louis.
Rezghi, A. (2025). Inattentiveness and the investment channel of monetary. *IMF Working Paper*, WP/25/25.
Rodríguez-Fuentes, C. J. (2006). *Regional monetary policy*. Routledge, Taylor & Francis Group.
Romer, P. M. (1990). Endogenous technological change. *Journal of Political Economy, 98*(5), S71–S102.
Sargent, T., & Wallace, N. (1975). "Rational" expectations, the optimal monetary instrument, and the optimal money supply rule. *Journal of Political Economy, 83*(2), 241–254.
Sargent, T. J., & Wallace, N. (1981). Some unpleasant monetarist arithmetic. *Federal Reserve Bank of Minneapolis Quarterly Review, 5*(Fall).
Taylor, J. B. (1980). Aggregate dynamics and staggered contracts. *Journal of Political Economy, 88*, 1–23.
Taylor, J. B. (1993). Discretion versus rules in practice. *Carnegie-Rochester Conference Series on Public Policy, 39*, 195–214.
Von Hagen, J. (2004). Hat die Geldmenge ausgedient? *Perspektiven der Wirtschaftspolitik, 5*(4), 423–453.
Yellen, J. (2016). Macroeconomic research after the crisis. Speech delivered at the Federal Reserve Bank of Boston, 14 October.

Chapter 3
Expanding Unequally and Unproductively

As argued in the preceding chapter, interregional inequality is an important feature of any development process. The U-shape hypothesis is not always corroborated by the evidence. There is also little consensus on the causes of interregional inequality, let alone policies that could significantly affect–improve or worsen–it. In part because of these reasons, social planners and policy makers are not too willing to accept any measures to address inequality if such measures create trade-offs with aggregate indicators based on the standard macro-framework. If the proposed measures to reduce inequality make national growth slower than the target or require changes (postponement) of predetermined national projects, they are not favored and put the proposed measures on the shelf even if the repercussions of the projects will widen the development gap between regions. This could happen either because they are not aware that those national projects could have some detrimental effects or because they insist that the projects must proceed no matter what.

There are intractable problems (hard to control) and rational despair that reflects hopelessness that arises from a logical assessment of a situation. For some social planners, interregional inequality may be considered intractable. If they accept that the problems of left-behind regions may have no solution or are still controversial, hence better focusing on other development issues and macroaggregates, they risk being seen as callous. On the other hand, pretending that all questions related to interregional inequality have clear answers is equally risky because if inequality persists it could be interpreted as they are incompetent. Between the two, there are social planners who are convinced that a clear solution to the problem is simply to allocate more resources in less developed regions.

What is the evidence? Did inequality between regions in Indonesia persist? By international standards, Indonesia's interregional inequality is high. But was it improving, stagnant, or worsening over time?

This chapter focuses on these questions. The evidence about the nature and extent of interregional inequality, including inequality in productivity is presented in the next Section. Its relation with Indonesia's structural transformation is discussed in

I. J. Azis, *Monetary Whispers Across Space*,
https://doi.org/10.1007/978-981-95-4625-1_3

the Section that follows. Our conjecture is that there is an important link between the country's structural transformation, productivity trends, and interregional inequality, based on which the role of the services sector and the presence of dualism are among the keys to understanding the country's high degree of interregional inequality.

3.1 Evidence

3.1.1 Towards Welfare Inequality

Common measures of inequality use statistical indicators such as the coefficient of variation and the Gini index. The latter was developed by statistician-cum-sociologist Corrado Gini in the early 1900s. His 1912 paper, written in Italian, "Variabilità e Mutuabilità," became known in the anglophone world only in 1921 through the exchange he had with Hugh Dalton, a British economist-cum-politician.[1] Calculated using data from individuals or households of income or wealth, the Gini index ranges from 0 to 1, where 0 represents perfect equality (everyone has the same income or wealth) and 1 represents perfect inequality (one person has all the income or wealth).

For inequality between regions, the most commonly used is the Williamson index. Since it is a population-weighted measure, the Williamson index is useful to compare the inequality between regions that have a different population size. Using the per capita gross regional domestic product (GRDP) data and measured along with the coefficient of variation, Indonesia has the highest degree of interregional inequality among countries of comparable size. For both measures, the numbers are close to 0.8 (Fig. 3.1). Although they are based on 2016 data, it is unlikely that the ranking has changed over the last few years. In fact, using a slightly altered formula, the Williamson index in Indonesia in 2023 is clearly higher than in 2016 (Fig. 3.2).

Using per capita personal consumption expenditure (PCE) data, the Williamson index is much higher and has increased more significantly, i.e., from 0.81 to 0.89. This level indicates a dramatic jump compared to what happened in 2000, when decentralization policy began in Indonesia. Notice also that the increase of the index is more persistent compared to the other two. Clearly, the inequality between regions has worsened since the decentralization policy was implemented.

Another important measure of interregional inequality is calculated based on labor productivity. As depicted in Fig. 3.2, the inequality of productivity fluctuated, dropping to below 0.7 in 2010, flattening to 2016 and increasing since then. This measure is more important to use because growth in productivity reflects the ability of the region to drive long-term economic expansion given the same

[1] Dalton was known for making an argument that transferring income from a richer person to a poorer person would increase overall social welfare. This transfer is known as the Pigou-Dalton transfer.

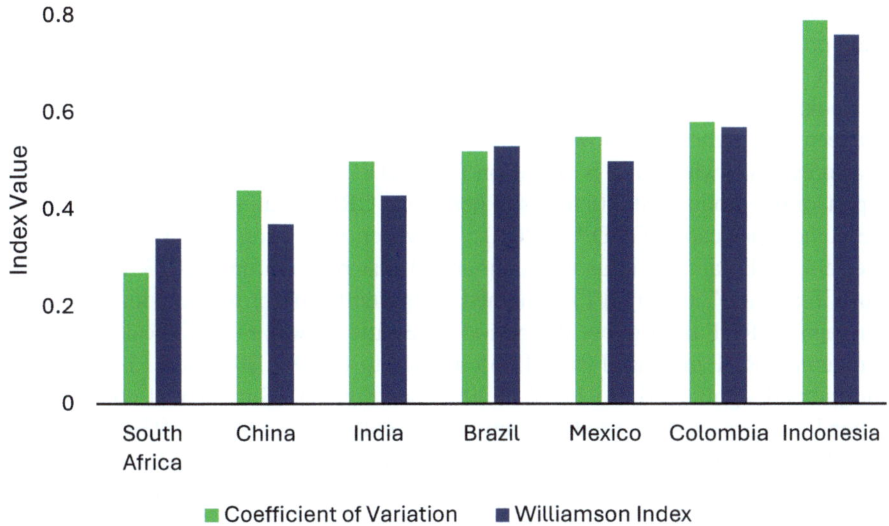

Fig. 3.1 Comparison of coefficient of variation and williamson index across countries. *Notes*: Indonesia (2016), Colombia & Mexico (2015), Brazil (2014), China & India (2013). *Source*: Taken from Azis (2022)

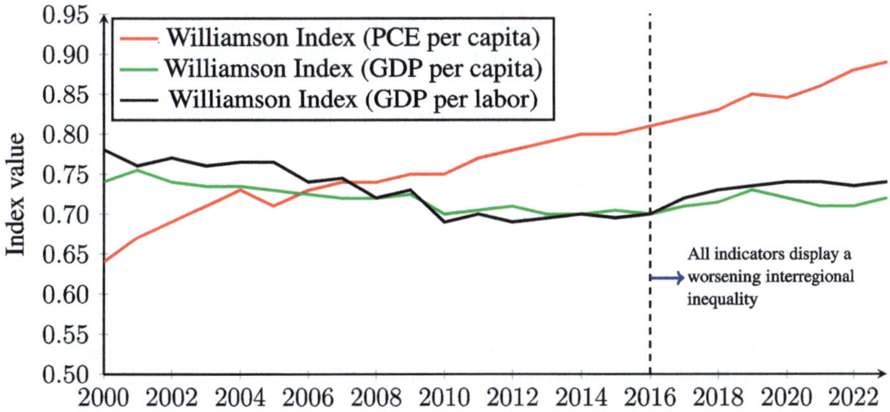

Fig. 3.2 Post-decentralization measures of interregional inequality in Indonesia. *Sources*: Author's calculation

factors proportions (sustainability aspect), to improve purchasing power and living standards (welfare aspect), to strengthen competitiveness (quality products and services aspect) and to increase efficiency of the use of inputs and other resources (environmental sustainability aspect). Any regional output growth cannot have a lasting impact without corresponding increases in productivity. The sustainability aspect is closely related to the hypothesis of endogenous growth theory, in which economic growth is determined by technological innovation, knowledge accumulation, and human capital development. These factors are mostly internal, and through them productivity can be elevated, creating a virtuous cycle of sustained economic growth.

Looking deeper at the distribution of welfare, more particularly based on the ratio between the highest and lowest level between regions, the worsening inequality is also evident, whether it is based on the GRDP per capita, the consumption per capita, or the productivity. In terms of per capita GRDP, Kalimantan Timur recorded the highest per capita GRDP in 2010.[2] However, beginning in 2015, DKI Jakarta overtook Kalimantan Timur and maintained that position until 2023. Meanwhile, Nusa Tenggara Timur (NTT) remained consistently the province with the lowest per capita GRDP throughout the period. The ratio between the highest and lowest per capita GRDP increased from 12.55 in 2010 to 12.89 in 2015 and 13.12 in 2020, and jumped significantly to 21.12 in 2023 (see Fig. 3.3). Similarly, if consumption expenditure per capita is used, the ratio persistently increased from 93.12 to 100.08 to 107.04 and 108.13, where DKI Jakarta consistently had the highest level and NTT the lowest (Fig. 3.4). The trend of the productivity ratio was not much different, except that there was a slight improvement between 2010 and 2015, before it continued to increase since then, and that the highest level in those years was in Kalimantan Timur, before being taken over by DKI Jakarta (Fig. 3.5). [3]

We can go into more details about the change in the ranking of other regions. In fact, the position of some regions in the ranking has changed, the most important reason being the changing share of the dominant sectors of the region, for example, the changing share oil and gas in Sumatera, Kalimantan, and some of the provinces in eastern Indonesia.

Some argue that what matters more are trends of convergence or divergence. When a group of regions made improvements in resource allocation and utilization, their efficiency also improved. If the number of such groups is fairly large, it is a sign that a convergence process is taking place.[4] There are also other alternative measures proposed to capture the degree of interregional inequality, some were developed to

---

[2] The high level in Kalimantan Timur was mainly driven by the mining and quarrying sector (coal, oil, and gas) and the agriculture and forestry sector (timber).

[3] The high level of productivity in Kalimantan Timur was mainly due to the region's small population size and richness in natural resources; i.e., timber (tropical forests), oil & gas, coal, and other minerals such as bauxite, nickel, and gold. However, in general terms, the high level of income and productivity per capita of the region did not attract many economic activities and people from other regions, a typical characteristic of the 'enclave economy' where only specific areas are dominated by a distinct and independent set of capital intensive industries, mainly mining and forest, operating independently of the broader local economy.

[4] There are different indicators of convergence. If the relationship between the initial level of per capita income and subsequent growth in regions is negative, it is a sign of 'β-convergence,' implying that poorer regions grow faster than richer ones. There are 2 types of 'β-convergence': if the negative relationship is derived without considering any conditioning factors, it is called 'absolute β convergence' and if it is derived after controlling for some conditions that affect the steady-state level of income, it is called 'conditional β convergence'. Another type of convergence is 'σ-convergence' which denotes the decreasing dispersion of per capita income between regions.

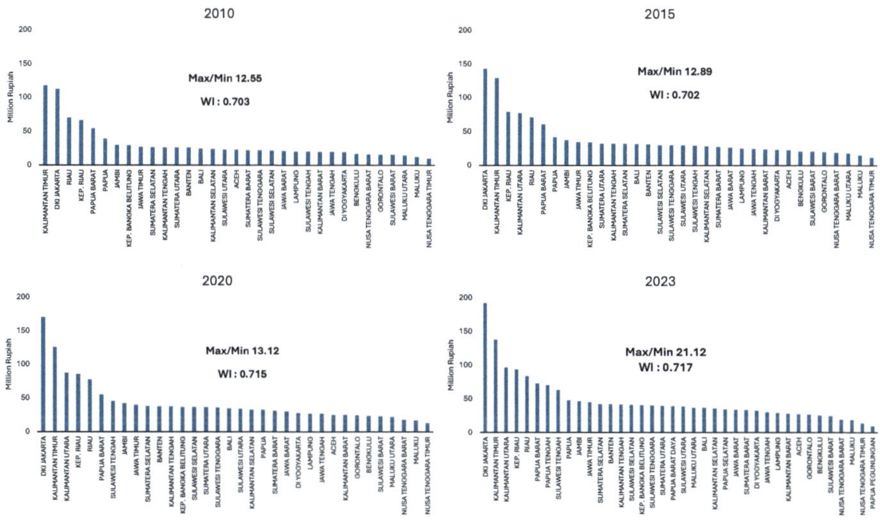

Fig. 3.3 Ranking of per-capita GRDP: 2010, 2015, 2020, 2023. *Source*: Author's calculation. *Notes*: Kalimantan Utara was officially established in 2012. However, BPS conducted back-casting, making Kalimantan Utara's data available from 2010 onwards

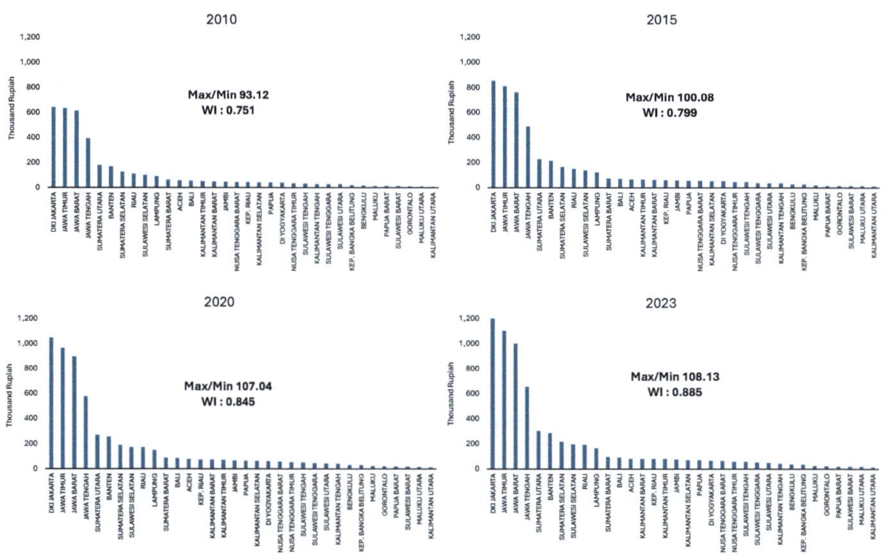

Fig. 3.4 Ranking of per-capita personal consumption expenditure: 2010, 2015, 2020, 2023. *Source*: Author's calculation. *Notes*: Kalimantan Utara was officially established in 2012. However, BPS conducted back-casting, making Kalimantan Utara's data available from 2010 onwards

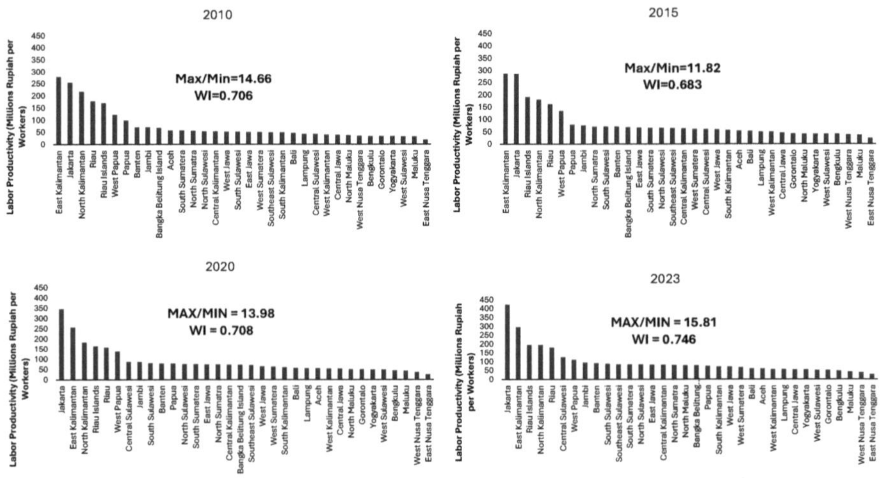

Fig. 3.5 Ranking of labor productivity: 2010, 2015, 2020, 2023. *Source*: Author's calculation. *Notes*: Kalimantan Utara was officially established in 2012. However, BPS conducted back-casting, making Kalimantan Utara's data available from 2010 onwards

help identify areas where social planners should focus on (essentially decomposing the measure), others were developed to make the measure more universal and meeting certain statistical properties.

However, no matter what alternative measures to use, the gap between the highest and lowest regions is still large, the multiple is more than 10 times, and it continues to increase. Most of the eastern parts of the country are lagged behind those in the western parts, especially Jawa. The only regions outside of Jawa that have a comparable ranking with Jawa are those that are rich in natural resources and low in population size. This spatial distribution is generally consistent with the outcome based on other welfare measures, including those related to health and education matters.

3.1.2 *Productivity: National and Regional Trends*

As a measure of regional welfare, productivity is superior to per-capita GRDP or consumption. This is particularly true when viewed from the perspectives of growth sustainability, people's standard of living, efficiency, competitiveness, and environmental sustainability. It is therefore important to look at trends in productivity and the productivity gap between regions.

However, some cautionary notes are in order. First, productivity is not a short-term indicator. The results of its improvements or deterioration may not be observable until several years to come. Official statistics likely miss the true picture and can give a false impression and conclusion. For example, when data on productivity do not show improvements after certain efforts and policies have been taken, one may jump to the conclusion that those efforts and policies do not work, or even wasteful. However, time lag may be the essence in a case where current spending and investment do not match the timely statistics on productivity. This classic problem of the 'productivity puzzle 2.0' occurred in some advanced economies in the 1970s and 1980s during the period of advances in information technology (IT) for microprocessors, personal computers, the Internet, and the mobile phone. Nobel laureate Robert Solow once remarked: "You can see the computer age everywhere but in the productivity statistics." Some also argued that productivity measures themselves do not catch up with technology, making those measures obsolete. There are also the problems of measurements. The point is that data on productivity should be treated with caution.

Total Factor Productivity (TFP) is a notable example. Although widely used, as it is considered a valuable tool for assessing aggregate productivity, it suffers from methodological and data drawbacks. Starting with a production function, TFP growth measures something that cannot be attributed to the accumulation of capital, labor, and other traditional inputs in the production function. It is known as the 'Solow residual'. The way it is calculated suffers from endogeneity problems that make the results distorted (i.e., simultaneous bias and sample selection bias).

In terms of data drawback, capital stock data, critically required to calculate TFP, are difficult to obtain. Even at the national level, they are often unavailable, let alone at the subnational regional level. The fact that different sectors and industries use a wide variety of inputs and produce diverse outputs also makes it difficult to generate standardized capital stock and consequently also an accurate measure of TFP. In a fast-changing technology environment, dynamic shifts in the industries can also create a mismatch, since TFP is essentially static. Thus, TFP should also be treated with caution. It may require continuous updating in both methodology and data, as the existing one may not be able to capture the true level of productivity.

To the extent that productivity is a measure of efficiency, comparing input use and output increase is a sensible way to do and use it for the evaluation. The incremental capital output ratio (ICOR) is one of such measures, where the numerator is the increase of capital stock and the denominator is the increase of output. It essentially shows how productive the use of capital in order to generate an increase in output is. That is, a high ICOR is a sign of inefficient capital use.

Looking at Indonesia's ICOR, the number was relatively high and continued to increase especially during the COVID pandemic, where the increase was dramatic because many businesses disappeared or reduced production, and most consumers cut their spending due to physical restrictions and the unpredictable nature of the crisis. At the same time, investment in some sectors, especially healthcare and digital infrastructure, increased rather significantly due to a growing need for remote activities, increased demand for healthcare to combat the crisis, behavioral shifts of people towards digital communication, and higher demand for online interactions. The disruptions in supply chains during the pandemic also led to a reduction in labor and production, while capital investment continued to increase. The stimulus package, introduced on all fronts, including expansionary fiscal and monetary

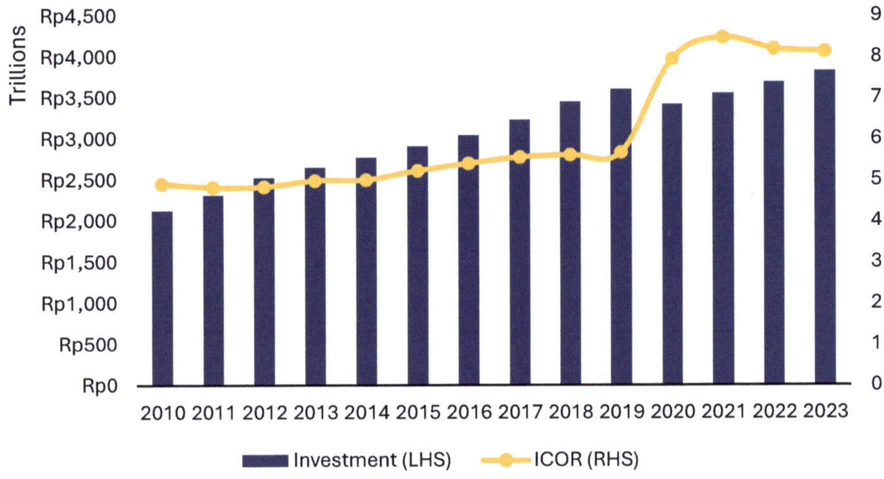

Fig. 3.6 Incremental capital output ratio (ICOR). *Source*: Author's calculation

policy, managed to prevent the recession from deepening. As physical restrictions were gradually lifted, the ICOR began to flatten in 2022. However, the relatively high level of ICOR speaks volumes about the country's level of efficiency and the enormous challenge to reverse the trend.

Compared to its regional peers, Indonesia's ICOR is high and growing (Fig. 3.6); the average ICORs in most emerging markets in Asia are approximately 4 to 5. This indicates a decline in investment efficiency. As shown in the figure, capital investment continues to increase as they are required to generate each unit of economic growth. The upward trend in ICOR also signals structural inefficiencies in capital allocation and a declining return on public and private investment. This reflects misaligned investment priorities, such as infrastructure projects that lack integration with productive sectors and the real need of most activities, or suffer from implementation delays. Under such circumstances, it would be harder to justify large-scale capital expenditures without structural reforms (institutional quality cannot keep pace with capital accumulation).

What about ICOR at the regional level? We calculated the ICOR for all regions, and the results show that the overall trends mimic that at the national level, i.e., high and in an upward trend (available upon request). The exceptions are in: Maluku Utara, Riau, Kepulauan Riau, and Papua, where the trends are fluctuating, and Jogyakarta, where it is relatively flat before slightly rising. The dramatic worsening is in Bali, where the ICOR surged very sharply, especially during the COVID pandemic. In fact, tourism in Bali was hardest hit during the pandemic. Based on the coefficient of variation between regions, the variability of ICOR increased from 0.39 in 2015 to 0.61 and 0.77 in 2020 and 2023, respectively. Those numbers are high by international standards and indicate that the level of efficiency (hence productivity) varies significantly between regions. It is important to note that the calculation of ICOR is sensitive to the assumptions being used about the depreciation rate and the

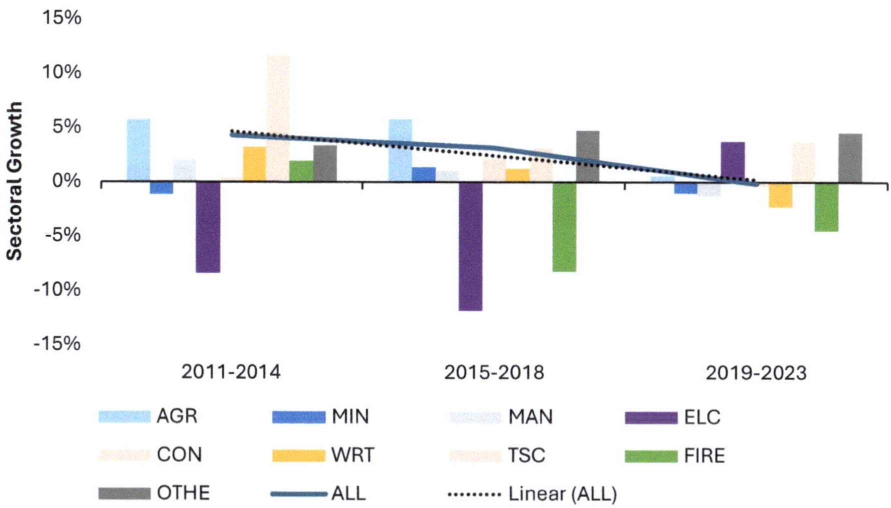

Fig. 3.7 Trends of labor productivity growth sector. *AGR* Agriculture, *MIN* Mining, *MAN* Manufacturing, *ELC* Electricity, *CON* Construction, *WRT* Trade Services, *TSC* Transport and Communication, *FIRE* Finance, Insurance, and Real Estate, *OTHE* Other Services. *Source*: Author's calculation

time lag, i.e., the time required before the investment generates output (here, we are assuming that the time lag is around 5 years).

For policy purposes, we need to discern the sources of variation. In this context, we use labor productivity and decompose its variations between components. We wish to measure the contribution of different components in causing the variability. Before doing so, let us first analyze the trend of Indonesia's labor productivity.

Figure 3.7 clearly shows that productivity growth in Indonesia is in a declining trend, where the most obvious was in the last decade or so. Taking 2015 as the initial point and grouping the periods into 2010–2015, 2016–2019, and 2020–2023, the fall was fairly dramatic, even reaching a negative growth in the last period. Only 3 of 9 sectors managed to avoid falling productivity.

Although most sectors still recorded positive growth in the first period (2010–2015), with the exception of the electricity (ELC) and construction (CON) sectors, there was a noticeable decrease in productivity growth during the period 2016–2019. During this time, the growth of aggregate productivity (labeled ALL in the figure) declined significantly, and four sectors (ELC, MIN, MAN and FIRE) experienced negative growth.

The downward trend deepened in the 2020–2023 period, with overall productivity growth (ALL) entering negative territory. Only three of nine sectors managed to sustain positive productivity growth: electricity (ELC), transportation and communication (TSC), and other services (OTHE). This indicates that the decline in productivity growth has become more widespread during the last decade, with the most severe contraction occurring during the most recent period.

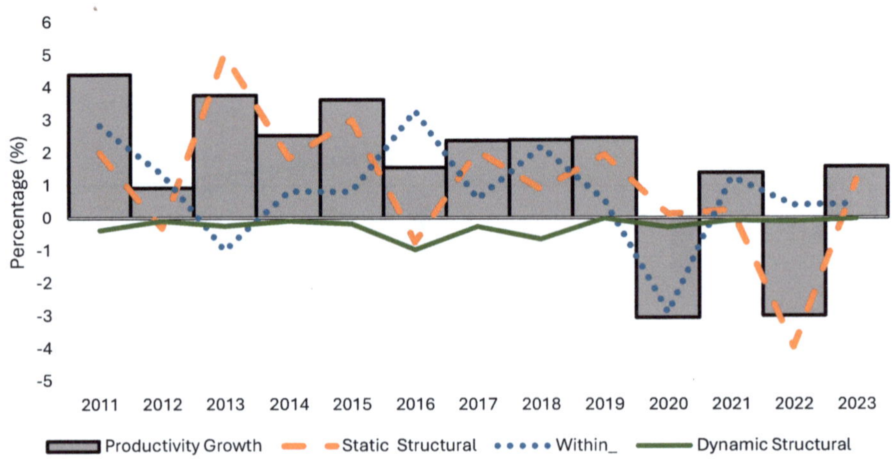

Fig. 3.8 Trends of labor productivity growth and its decomposition. *Source*: Based on author's calculation

Breaking down the components, Fig. 3.8 shows the results of the decomposition. The trend line clearly points to a persistent decline in the last decade. Negative growth is expected in 2020 and 2022, due to the unprecedented shock caused by the COVID pandemic. But even if hypothetically that shock did not occur, it is hard to imagine that the declining pattern would have been reversed. In 2023, the productivity growth jumped, reaching a higher level than in 2021, strictly due to the low base in 2022.

It is also important to note that any productivity data that show an increase during COVID could give a false impression that efficiency has improved. As discussed in Azis (2024), the severity and broad-based nature of the COVID shock caused many small businesses to suffer from outright losses of employment and a sharp decline in work hours, more than what larger firms had experienced. The decline in work hours among small businesses reached 14–17% compared to less-than 9% in larger firms during the early stage of the pandemic (ILO, 2021). Since average productivity is measured by the ratio of value added over work hours or over the number of workers, that ratio increased significantly during the pandemic, giving a false impression that productivity had increased. The fact is that the increase was driven by a sharp decline in the denominator, not improvements in efficiency.

With that onset, the results of the decomposition show that both the 'within' and the 'static structural' components fluctuated. In general, they dominated the overall productivity trends of the country. The "within" or intra-sectoral component measures how efficiently resources are used within a specific sector. It involves both types of input, tangible (equipment of technological advancements) and intangible (better skill and management). The 'static structural' component, on the other hand, captures the impact of structural changes, where productivity changes are driven by the reallocation of resources across different sectors within an economy.

Productivity improvements will increase if workers and production move from low- to high-productivity sectors. As Fig. 3.8 shows, the contribution of these two components fluctuated, in some years they provided a positive contribution, in others they dragged down productivity growth. However, both components did not provide sufficient information for us to gauge the prospect of sustaining growth in the future. This is where the 'dynamic structural' component is useful to track down.

It is clear from the figure that the contribution of the 'dynamic structural' component has never been positive, implying that workers and production in Indonesia had not moved to sectors whose productivity was increasing. Even if some of them managed to move to higher-productivity sectors, the productivity of those very sectors was stagnant or declining. Various factors may have caused this outcome, ranging from a lack of skill and technological advancement, uncertainty in regulations, limited human resources, or skill mismatches. All of these factors interact in complex ways. In any case, the trend clearly suggests that the structural transformation process in Indonesia did not bring with it improvements in productivity.

What about regional productivity trends? Based on the decomposition results in every single region (see Appendix 3.1), the general picture is not different from those derived from regional ICOR, except that here we can identify the components that caused the declining trend. Most of the productivity growth was driven by the 'within' component, although during some years the largest contributor in some regions was the 'static component.' In fact, from a productivity perspective, many poor regions in Indonesia are in a grim position. They suffer from the inadequacy of appropriate infrastructure, making it difficult, especially for small businesses and home industries, to perform well. Limited opportunities have also prevented them from shifting to higher-productivity jobs.

There is clearly a productivity gap between regions, but how large is the gap? What is the trend over time and what are the main determinants of it? Was the variability in productivity across regions due to regional differences in industry mix, misallocation of resources, or was it purely due to differences in productivity level? To answer these questions, we need to decompose the variance of regional productivity shown in Fig. 3.2 earlier.

Of several decomposition techniques, we use the one that ensures the invariability of the coefficient when the productivity in every region is changed by the same proportion (*scale independence* property).[5] Applied to Indonesian data, the trend

[5] This is one of the important properties of inequality measure, which keeps the coefficient-of-variation remains invariant if the productivity in every region is changed by the same proportion. In particular, we use the following squared employment-weighted coefficient of variation ($COV_w{}^2$):

$$\mathrm{COV}_w^2 = \alpha + \beta + \gamma + 2\delta + 2\varepsilon + 2\phi$$

where α = industry mix differential component, β = allocative efficiency differential component, γ = productivity differential component, and the remaining three parts denote the covariance of $\alpha\beta$, $\alpha\gamma$, and $\beta\gamma$. The other properties, that is, population independence, anonymity and the Pigou-Dalton transfer principle, are all met by the specification COV_w^2.

of each component is shown in Fig. 3.9. Of the three components, the variation between regions was primarily driven by the productivity component (β). Although fluctuating, this component was always the largest and has increased since 2016. Hence, based only on this criterion, Indonesia's interregional inequality in sectoral productivity has worsened. Since investment in infrastructure usually plays a significant role in driving productivity improvements and that the observed trend is the result of accumulated past investments within a given sector, this suggests that most investment in infrastructure, especially after 2016, was directed disproportionately toward already high-productivity regions, presumably in Jawa and other resource-rich regions. As shown in Fig. 3.10, this was indeed the case and the interregional inequality also got worse as indicated by the increase in the coefficient of variation from 0.591 to 0.682.

On the one hand, this could be due to efficiency consideration; on the other hand, it also indicates a lack of priority to reduce the productivity gap between developed and less developed regions. We offer two possible explanations for this: first, enhancing productivity was not on the top agenda of the social planner due, among other things, to the long time required to experience the benefits. The priority was surely overtaken by maximizing output growth. Second, interregional inequality was not a major concern for the government during that period. The slowing national growth was.

The allocative efficiency component fluctuated, but it was always larger than the industry mix component (see again Fig. 3.9). This indicates that some regions

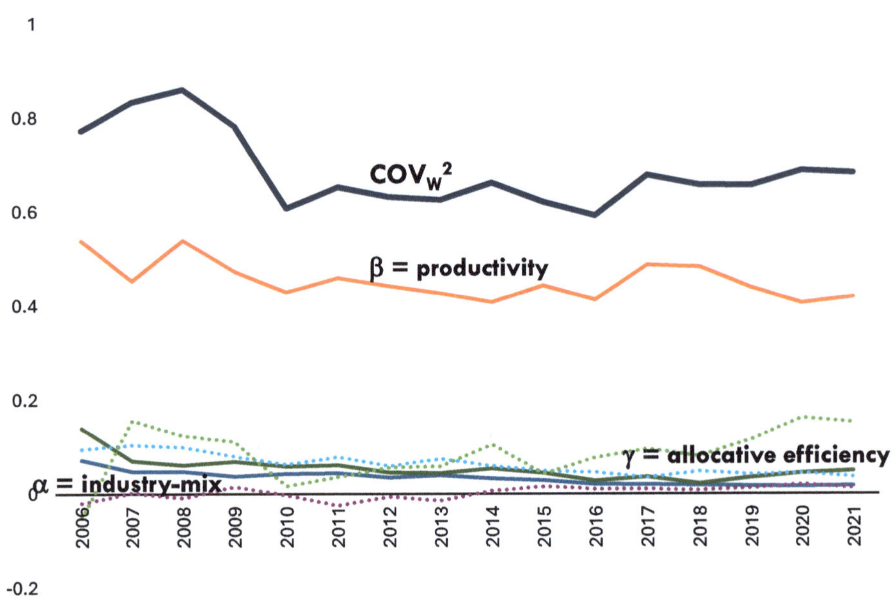

Fig. 3.9 Decomposition results of inequality in labor productivity. *Source*: Based on Author's calculation

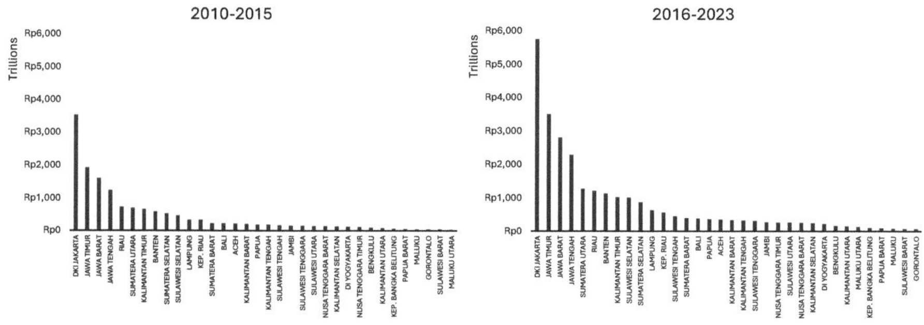

Fig. 3.10 Regional investment distribution in Indonesia (Constant price, 2010=100). *Source*: Author's calculation

still clearly faced serious challenges in their efforts to improve efficiency. The contribution of the allocative efficiency component to the overall inequality of productivity also increased slightly since 2016. The fact that the industry mix component had the lowest contribution suggests that the sectoral structure between regions was not the culprit for Indonesia's interregional inequality. Improved diversification in some regions could surely help, but it would be able to reduce the gap between developed and less developed regions.

Having learned about the trends, the extent and nature of productivity, nationally and regionally, and also its variability between regions, it is of interest to find out if there were fundamental factors that could explain why the Indonesian economy produced such an outcome. More specifically, are there particular activities or sectors that played an important role in generating the country's low and falling growth of productivity? As it turns out, the structural transformation or the changing dynamics of the sectoral structure holds the key to many of these issues. The bulk of discussions in the next Section are devoted to this subject.

3.2 Growing Without Productivity

The first part of this Section looks at the sectoral structure of the Indonesian economy, in which the services sector gained its dominance. The subsequent part discusses the link between that structure and the poor productivity performance of the country in which dualism prevails.

3.2.1 Sectoral Transformation and Dualism

Sectoral patterns of development refer to the economic transition from primary (agriculture) to secondary (primarily manufacturing) and tertiary (primarily services). The standard arguments behind the process are fairly straightforward. As income grows, so does demand for goods and services. Through innovation and other technological advances, labor and other resources will be reallocated to the production of manufacturing and services, which are often located in urban areas. The required skills are acquired through training and education, which is another type of service. Given that there are capacities to generate surpluses, some products are exported, and given the rising income from the new sectors and also due to efficiency consideration, imports may also increase. To reduce reliance on only selected products, we have made attempts to diversify production. This will generate more jobs with different skill requirements. As people's preference shifts towards more diverse and higher-quality products and services, a diversification process takes place in both production and consumption.

This is more-or-less the mechanism behind the sectoral patterns of development leading towards higher income. Two phenomena are embedded in the mechanism: growing urbanization to facilitate resource reallocation and greater efficiency to make the economy more productive. Urbanization reflects the forces of concentration or agglomeration as discussed in the previous chapter. However, in most discussions about development strategy, this phenomenon rarely takes center stage. By concentrating in urban areas or agglomerating in center locations, numerous benefits are acquired that enable activities to be more productive, e.g., economies of scale, low transport costs, knowledge sharing, and all kinds of networking (Romer, 1990). However, like agglomeration, productivity is hardly the focal point of conventional analysis. It is often undermined in policy discussions. The predominant thinking is always output growth.

The symbiotic relationship between agglomeration (spatial phenomena) and productivity is critical in the analysis of development patterns. The implied allocation of resources includes a process in which resources are increasingly directed toward more productive and profitable activities. Hence, a shift from agriculture to manufacturing and services without improvements in productivity is not what structural transformation is all about. If it were, it would have been fragmentary, misleading, or simply a flawed concept.

Even if global data show a close association between sectoral shift and improved productivity, it is misleading to make a generalization of cross-sectional observations. Distinguishing advanced and non-advanced economies, the role of services sector in structural transformation could defy the association. In advanced economies, most services consist of highly productive activities such as telecommunications, financial sector, and business services. But in many developing countries, the bulk of services is in the trade sector, especially retail trade, the value-added of which is relatively low but the number of people working in the sector is very high. As the sector's share in total output increases due to the increase in the number of units, not the increase in value added per unit, the sector's low labor productivity decreases further, lowering overall national productivity.

Described in Figs. 3.11 and 3.12, Indonesia's services sector has been dominant in terms of both value added share and employment share, except in 2010 where the

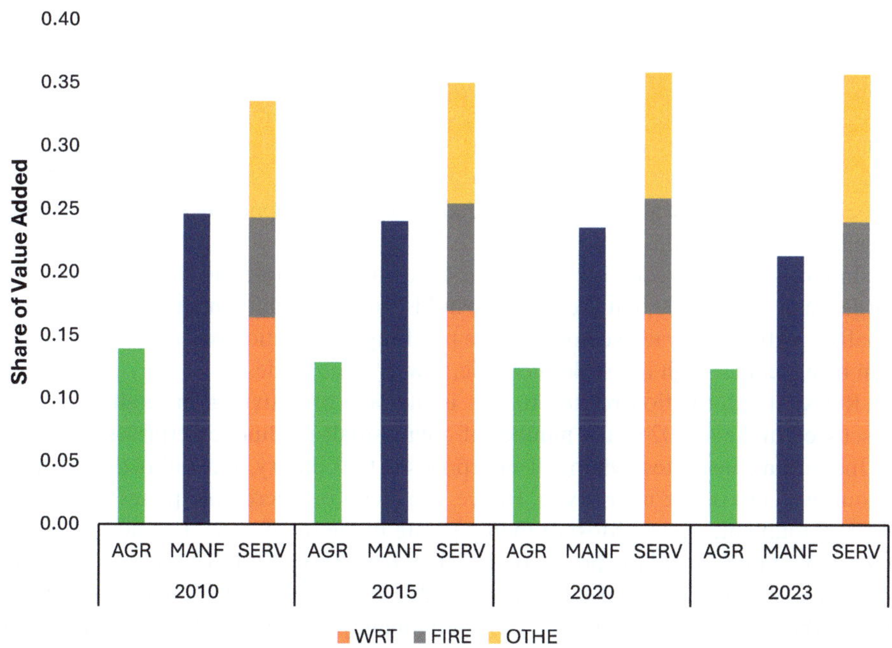

Fig. 3.11 Share of value-added in agriculture (AGR), Manufacturing (MANF) & Services (SERV). *Notes*: The services sector includes Trade (WRT), Finance, Insurance and Real Estate (FIRE), and Other Services (OTHE). *Source*: Based on Author's calculation

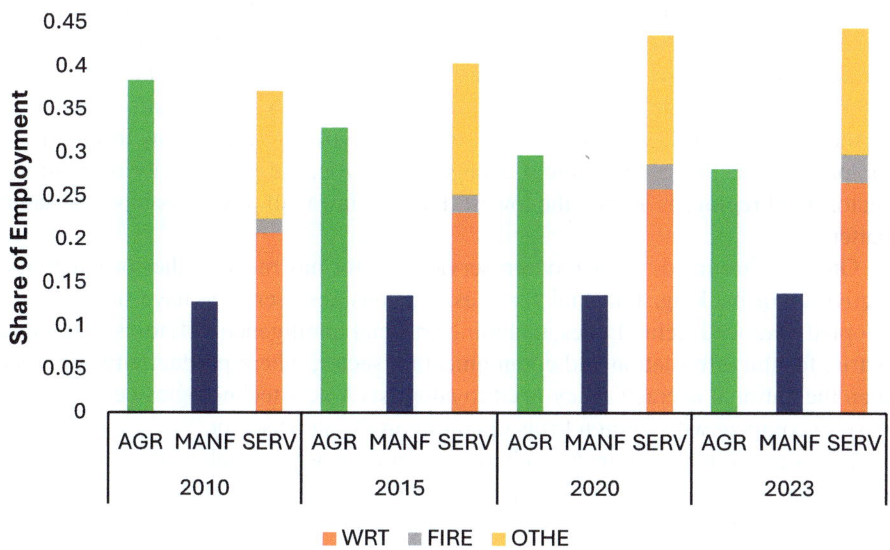

Fig. 3.12 Share of Employment in Agriculture (AGR), Manufacturing (MANF)& Services (SERV). *Notes*: The services sector includes Trade (WRT), Finance, Insurance and Real Estate (FIRE), and Other Services (OTHE). *Source*: Based on Author's calculation

employment share was still dominated by the agricultural sector. Within services, the trade sector is the largest. Note that the Indonesian statistical office does not separate retail trade from wholesale trade because trade data are not collected through surveys; instead, the office uses a commodity flow approach where the difference between commodity price at the consumers and producers level is used, including the trade and margin components (data for the latter are obtained from special surveys). The sector's value added is derived by applying such an approach to all tradable activities.

In terms of value added per unit of establishment, wholesale trade is obviously larger than retail trade, but the opposite holds true for employment. Hence, there is dualism within the trade sector, and the resulting distribution of labor productivity can be expected: high in wholesale trade, low in retail trade.

Relevant information related to this is the size of activities in retail trade. As discussed in Azis (2024), the number of micro-small-medium enterprises (MSME) in Indonesia constitutes 99% of all enterprises in the country, and within that number about 99% are of the micro type. Hence, the share of micro enterprises is roughly 98% of total enterprises. Most of them operate in the retail trade. It is no secret that these companies have low productivity. They have faced all kinds of problems and obstacles, causing many of them to be unable to repay credits they received from banks (high nonperforming loans and delinquency) and prevent them from being able to raise productivity.

Indeed, the productivity of trade sector is among the lowest in the economy. Millions of small retail trade units, including informal enterprises, are spread throughout the country, from Aceh to Papua, engaging in diverse activities such as street vending; open-air market stalls typically operating in traditional wet markets; kiosks selling daily necessities such as soap, cigarettes, and sachet water; informal grocery stores (warungs); and other outlets mostly individual or family-run with limited stock, no formal accounting, and participation in petty trade in perishables. As depicted in Fig. 3.13, their productivity was not only low but also decreased further since 2015. Upon careful examination, in virtually all regions in Indonesia the pattern was the same. Without a single exception, the productivity of the trade sector in all regions is among the lowest. Even in Jawa, all provinces have the same patterns:

On the other hand, other modern services sector has much higher productivity. Activities in banking, financial services, and business services have increasingly adopted advanced technologies, including artificial intelligence (AI) tools. The same is true for the information and communication sector, where productivity is higher than the national average. They need to adopt such new technologies because they have to compete with foreign firms operating in the same sector.

Given rapid advances in AI technology, an increasing number of modern businesses, including foreign firms operating in Indonesia, have increasingly adopted these technologies. Although domestic firms can leverage local knowledge and relationships with customers better and more able to take advantage of government programs and supports, they are always under pressure to do more innovative ways

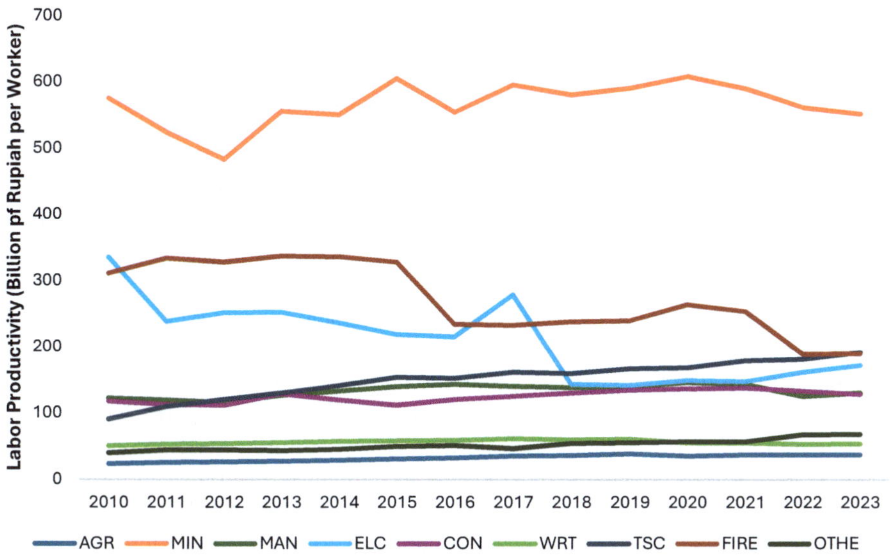

Fig. 3.13 Sectoral labor productivity sector. *AGR* Agriculture, *MIN* Mining, *MAN* Manufacturing, *ELC* Electricity, *CON* Construction, *WRT* Trade Services, *TSC* Transport and Communication, *FIRE* Finance, Insurance, and Real Estate, *OTHE* Other Services. *Source*: Based on Author's calculation

to keep the business afloat and compete with foreign players. For some who can afford, adopting new technologies is the only solution. With new technologies, they can deal with data and information more accurately, analyze market trends and consumer feedback quickly to identify gaps and opportunities, provide instant and better customer support, reduce operational costs, and automate mundane tasks. For banks and other financial institutions, the use of AI can help detect unusual patterns that can be caused by fraudulent activities, especially when the use of digital banking and digital money is widespread. All of these help improve their productivity. Many small businesses, especially those in less developed regions in eastern Indonesia, cannot afford to use such technologies. This dualism in services has contributed to the anomaly in the country's structural transformation: a growing share of services but with a decreasing growth in productivity.[6]

[6] Dualism is equally rampant in certain manufacturing activities where more variety of tools with advanced technologies are available, e.g., cloud computing for data storage and processing capabilities, artificial intelligence (AI) and machine learning (ML) for quality control and manufacturing process optimization, robots and automated systems for assembly and packaging, and 3D Printing for creating complex products with reduced waste. Some Indonesian manufacturers have used these tools, while many small and medium manufacturers cannot afford to buy/use them.

3.2.2 *Unproductive Expansion*

Another way to evaluate the structural transformation and its anomaly is by looking at whether the growing sectors in the economy are those that experience improved productivity.

Figure 3.14 summarizes trends during the last decade, where the *x* axis denotes the change in the share of employment of the sector and the *y* axis denotes the relative growth of the sector's productivity compared to the national average (measured by the logarithm of sectoral productivity/total productivity). Anything on the right (left) side of the vertical zero line indicates an increase (decrease) of employment share, and anything above (below) the horizontal zero line indicates productivity growth higher (lower) than the national average. The solid circles and lines refer to 2011–2016 and the dotted circles and lines are for 2016–2023.

Let us look at the 3 main sectors, that is, agriculture (AGR), manufacturing (MFG) and services consisting of Trade (WRT), Finance, Insurance and Real Estate (FIRE), Transport & Communication (TSC), Accommodation & Restaurant (ACC), and Other Services (OTH). The share of labors working in the agricultural sector continued to fall, as did its relative productivity. In the case of the manufacturing sector (MFG), the employment share slightly increased (consistent with what is shown in Fig. 3.12) and the relative productivity continued to be higher than the national average, although less than during 2011–2016. Within the services sector, where most Indonesian workers work, trends varied.

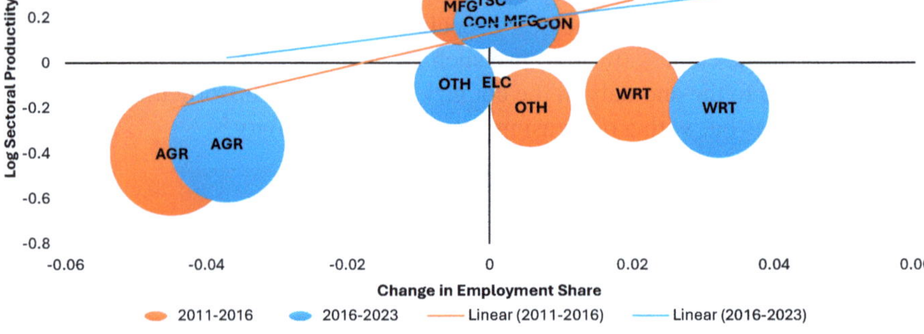

Fig. 3.14 Dynamics of sectoral employment share and relative productivity. *Source*: Based on Author's calculation

If we look at the largest subsector within services, trade (WRT), the share clearly increased but its relative productivity declined. During 2011–2016, productivity was already lower than average and worsened in 2016–2023. For other services (OTH), which consisted of a variety of services, including transport, accommodation, and restaurant, the relative productivity continued to be lower than the average, although in 2016–2023 the gap narrowed. But the employment share in this sub-sector declined. As expected, the finance, insurance and real estate sector (FIRE) continued to register higher and increasing productivity than average. However, the growth of its employment share fell, reaching close to the no-growth line. Automation and the adoption of some advanced technologies in this sector may have contributed to the deceleration.

The way Fig. 3.14 was drawn provides another useful observation. Imagine if most sectors experienced an increase in both employment share and relative productivity. Even if some continued to suffer from lower relative productivity than average, the gap will narrow. Depending on where the positions of the circles in the figure are, in this hypothetical scenario, if we draw a trend line, the slope would be positive. In contrast, if most sectors increase their share of employment but with a decrease in relative productivity compared to the average, the slope of the trend line would be negative. Obviously, the larger the positive slope, the better the prospect of productivity in the economy would be. Vice versa, the steeper the negative slope, the grimmer the prospect.

The trend lines for two periods in Fig. 3.14 are both positive, implying that Indonesia still has the opportunity to improve productivity through structural transformation. The challenge is not as severe as in the case when the slope is negative. However, the bad news is that, the positive slope has gotten smaller since 2016, suggesting that the opportunity has been narrowing. If the trend continues and remains unattended, it is possible that the country will fail to sustain even moderate growth in the coming years. Regionally, some variations are observed in terms of location, movements of each sector, and slope of the trend line. Some regions experienced improvements by showing a reverse slope from negative to positive during the two periods under study, for example, Bali, Kalimantan Selatan, Kalimantan Timur, Kepulauan Riau, Lampung, Sulawesi Tenggara and Sulawesi Utara and Sumatera Utara. However, more regions experienced a deterioration, where the slope shifted from positive to negative, for example, Aceh, Bengkulu, Kalimantan Barat, Riau, Sulawesi Barat, Sumatera Barat, and Jawa Barat. More concerning, almost all regions in eastern Indonesia experienced a deterioration; e.g., Maluku, NTB, NTT, and Papua (see Appendix 3.2).

Realizing the importance of retail trade in Indonesia's productivity trends, despite the unavailability of retail trade data, we used the sectoral breakdown data of Indonesia's input-output (IO) tables for the corresponding years. Using the same share of retail trade in total trade from those IO tables, we generate the estimated value-added of retail trade (RTL). Figure 3.15 shows the results. However, because IO tables are produced only in selected years, we need to adjust the periodization;

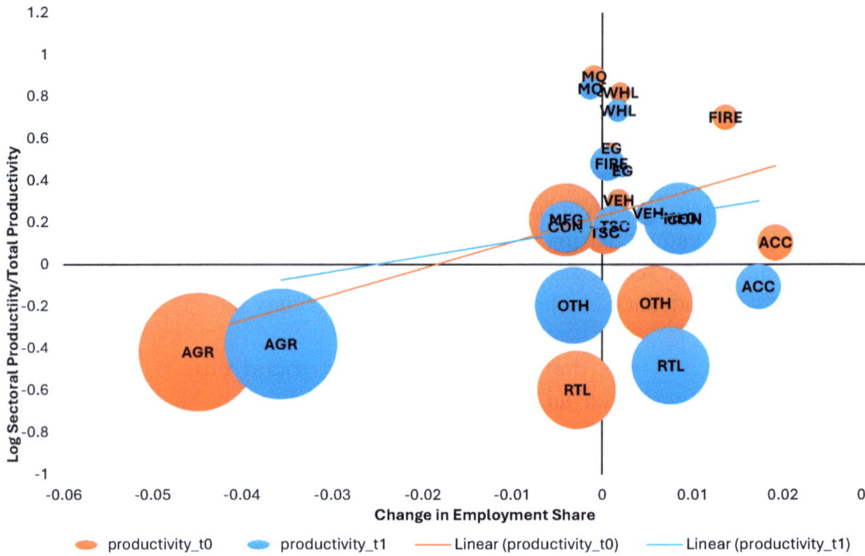

Fig. 3.15 Dynamics of sectoral employment share and relative productivity (with retail trade). *Source*: Based on Author's calculation. *Notes*: t0 = 2011–2016; t1= 2016 to the latest year of IO publication

therefore, Figs. 3.14 and 3.15 are not exactly comparable. However, the overall trends and conclusions remain intact.

The fall in employment share with persistent decline in relative productivity of the agriculture and other services sectors and the stagnant share with increased productivity in the manufacturing sector are clearly observed. But our concern is more with the retail trade sector (RTL). Compared to the overall trade (WRT) that includes wholesale trade, the increase in share or RTL was more dramatic, that is, it reverted from a fall in 2011–2016 to an increase in share in 2016–2023. Yet, in both cases the relative productivity continued to fall.

Therefore, whether using an absolute or relative number, the evidence is clear: Being the largest labor-absorbing and fast-growing activities, retail trade in Indonesia suffers from low and falling productivity. This contributes significantly to the persistent fall in the country's overall productivity growth (see Fig. 3.8 again). In short, Indonesia's structural transformation did not bring with it an improvement in productivity growth. The deceleration occurred persistently since the early 2000s, made a brief pause in the first half of the last decade, resumed since 2016 despite massive investment in infrastructure, and got worse during the COVID pandemic.

Appendix 3.1: Regional Labor Productivity

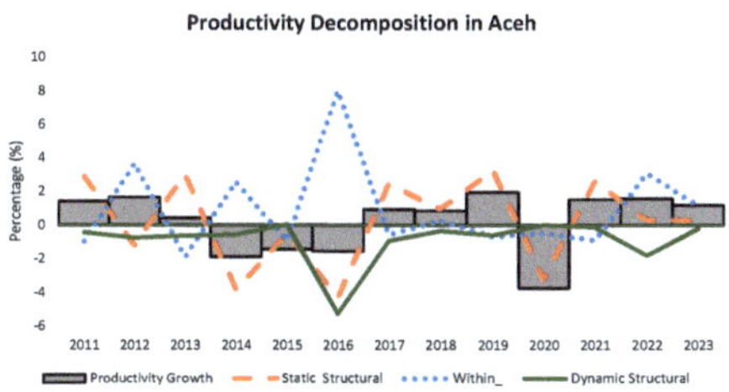

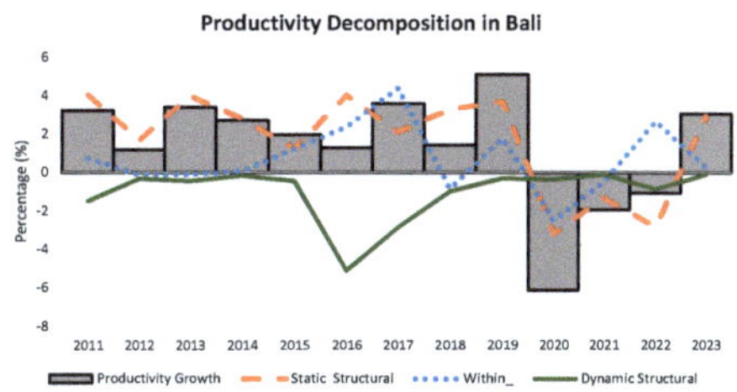

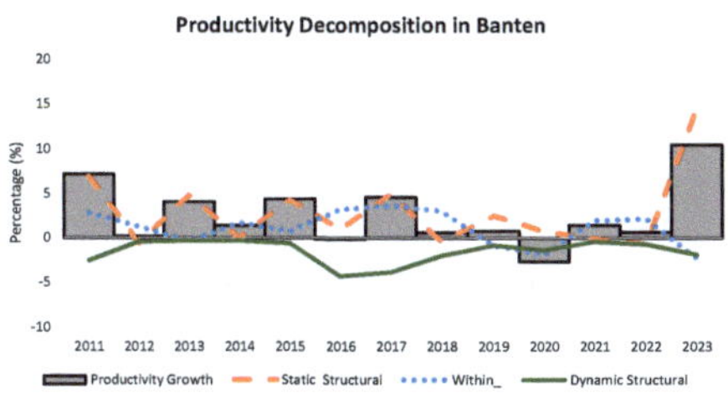

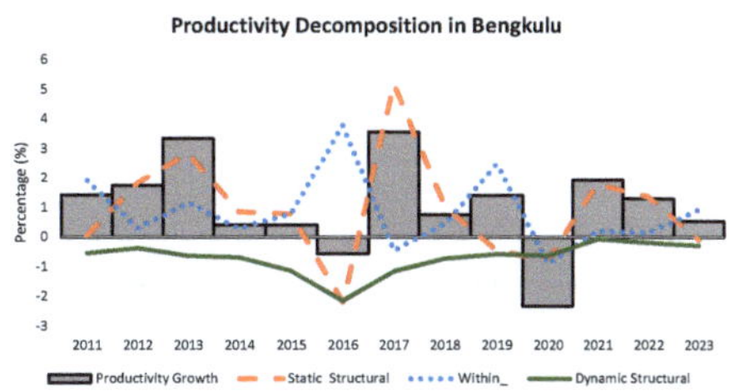

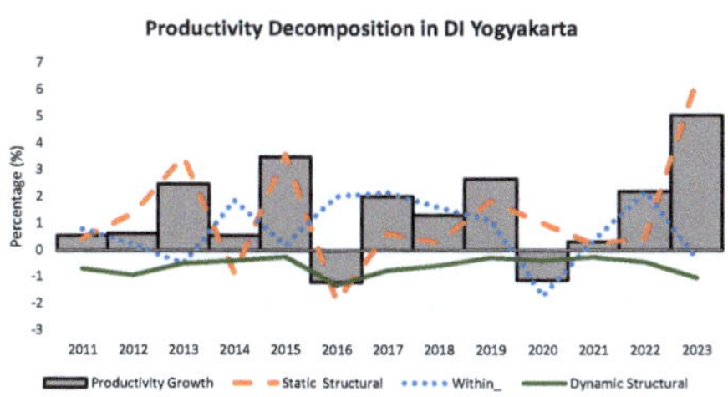

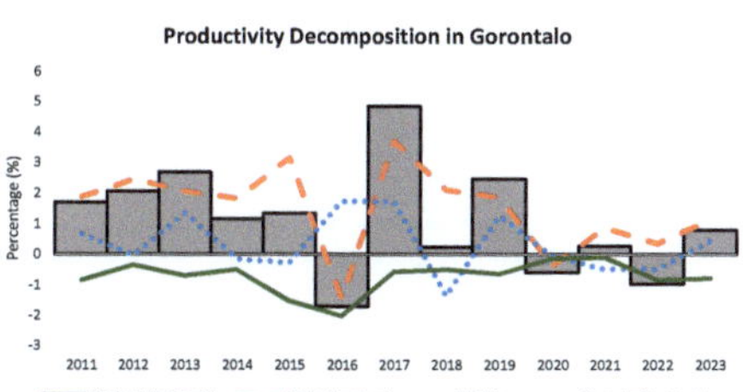

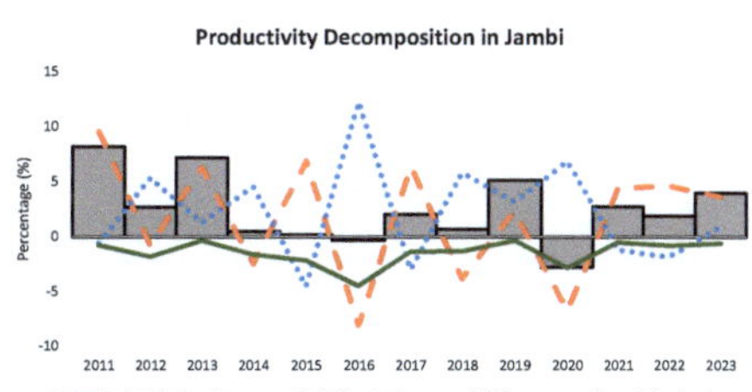

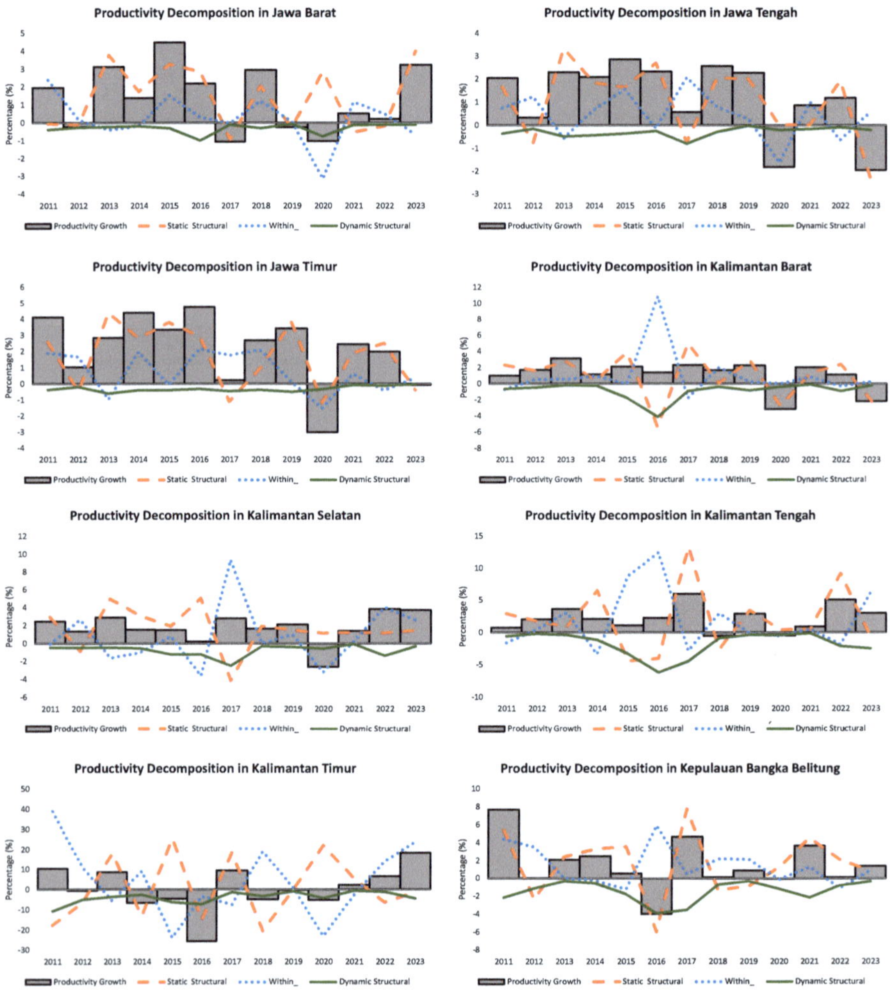
Productivity Decomposition in Jawa Barat
Productivity Decomposition in Jawa Tengah
Productivity Decomposition in Jawa Timur
Productivity Decomposition in Kalimantan Barat
Productivity Decomposition in Kalimantan Selatan
Productivity Decomposition in Kalimantan Tengah
Productivity Decomposition in Kalimantan Timur
Productivity Decomposition in Kepulauan Bangka Belitung
Percentage (%)
2011 2012 2013 2014 2015 2016 2017 2018 2019 2020 2021 2022 2023
Productivity Growth
Static Structural
Within_
Dynamic Structural

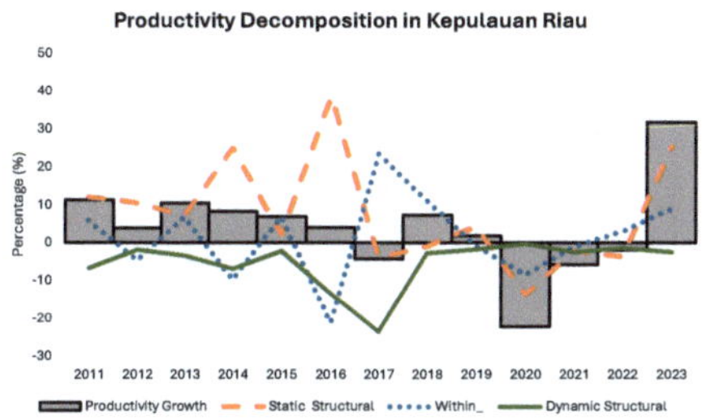
Productivity Decomposition in Kepulauan Riau
Percentage (%)
50 40 30 20 10 0 -10 -20 -30
2011 2012 2013 2014 2015 2016 2017 2018 2019 2020 2021 2022 2023
Productivity Growth
Static Structural
Within_
Dynamic Structural

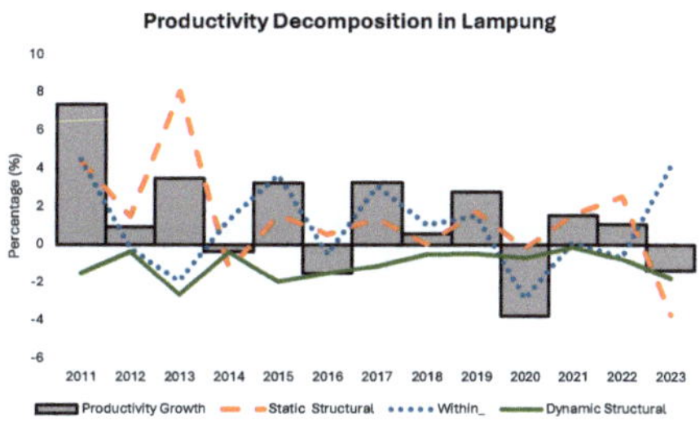
Productivity Decomposition in Lampung
Percentage (%)
10 8 6 4 2 0 -2 -4 -6
2011 2012 2013 2014 2015 2016 2017 2018 2019 2020 2021 2022 2023
Productivity Growth
Static Structural
Within_
Dynamic Structural

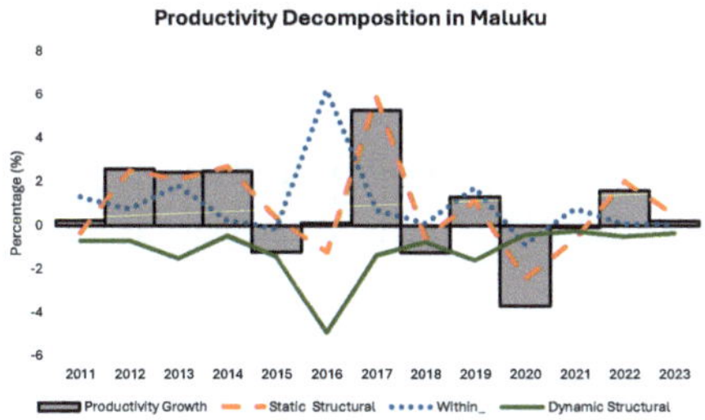
Productivity Decomposition in Maluku
Percentage (%)
8 6 4 2 0 -2 -4 -6
2011 2012 2013 2014 2015 2016 2017 2018 2019 2020 2021 2022 2023
Productivity Growth
Static Structural
Within_
Dynamic Structural

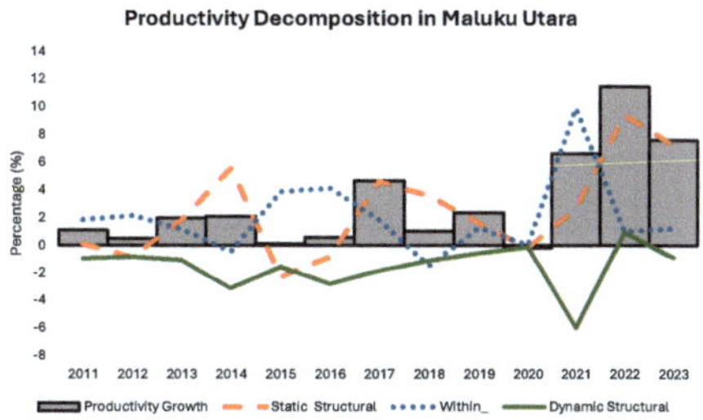
Productivity Decomposition in Maluku Utara
Percentage (%)
14 12 10 8 6 4 2 0 -2 -4 -6 -8
2011 2012 2013 2014 2015 2016 2017 2018 2019 2020 2021 2022 2023
Productivity Growth
Static Structural
Within_
Dynamic Structural

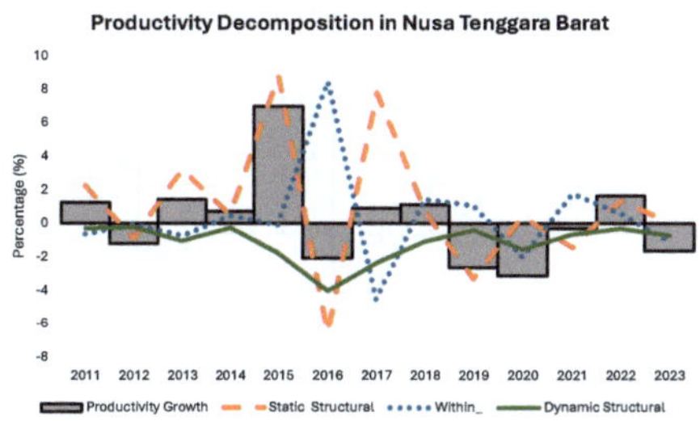
Productivity Decomposition in Nusa Tenggara Barat
Percentage (%)
10 8 6 4 2 0 -2 -4 -6 -8
2011 2012 2013 2014 2015 2016 2017 2018 2019 2020 2021 2022 2023
Productivity Growth
Static Structural
Within_
Dynamic Structural

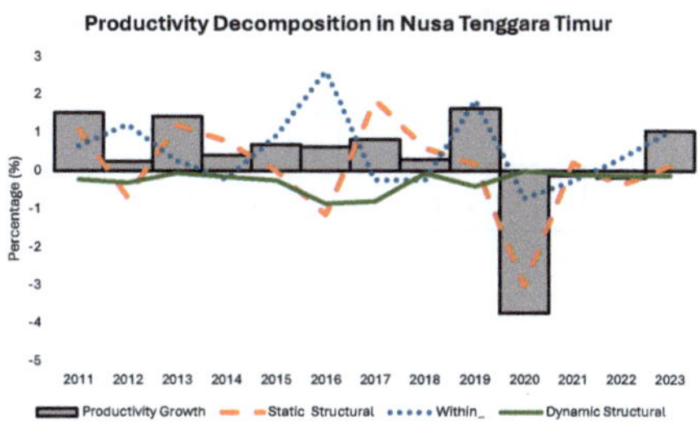
Productivity Decomposition in Nusa Tenggara Timur
Percentage (%)
3 2 1 0 -1 -2 -3 -4 -5
2011 2012 2013 2014 2015 2016 2017 2018 2019 2020 2021 2022 2023
Productivity Growth
Static Structural
Within_
Dynamic Structural

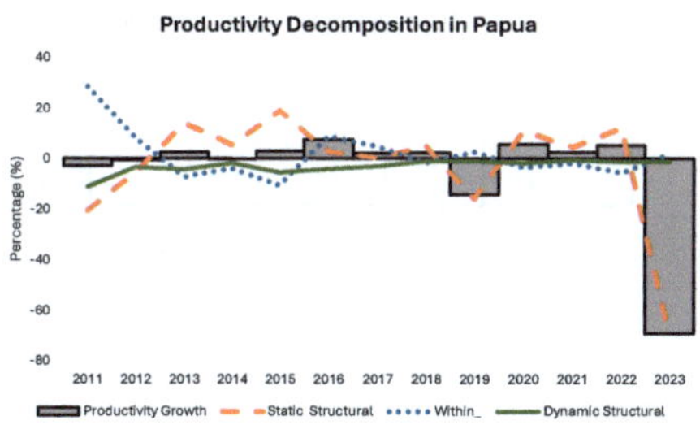
Productivity Decomposition in Papua
Percentage (%)
40 20 0 -20 -40 -60 -80
2011 2012 2013 2014 2015 2016 2017 2018 2019 2020 2021 2022 2023
Productivity Growth
Static Structural
Within_
Dynamic Structural

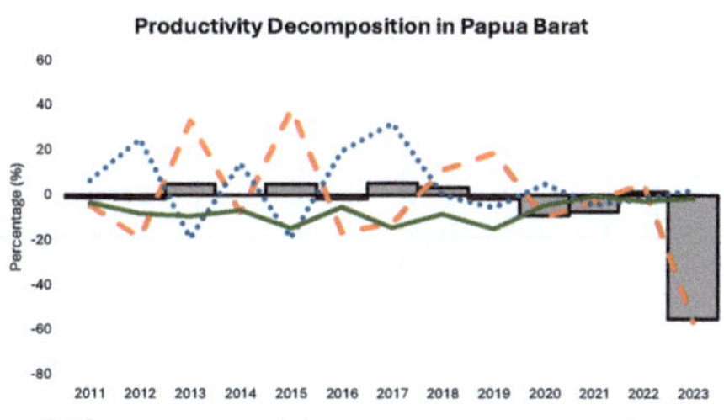
Productivity Decomposition in Papua Barat
Percentage (%)
60 40 20 0 -20 -40 -60 -80
2011 2012 2013 2014 2015 2016 2017 2018 2019 2020 2021 2022 2023
Productivity Growth
Static Structural
Within_
Dynamic Structural

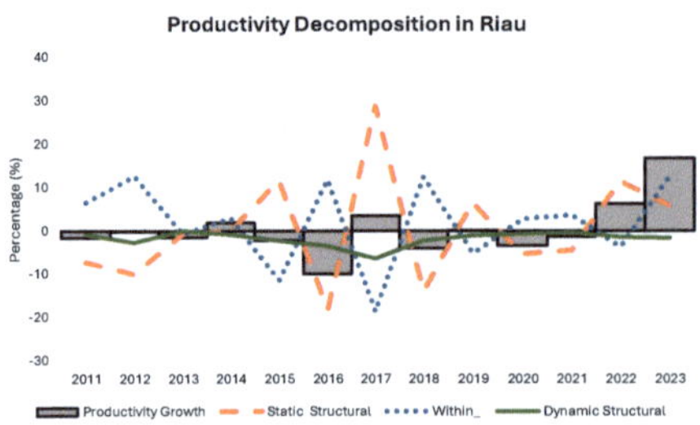
Productivity Decomposition in Riau
Percentage (%)
2011 2012 2013 2014 2015 2016 2017 2018 2019 2020 2021 2022 2023
Productivity Growth
Static Structural
Within_
Dynamic Structural

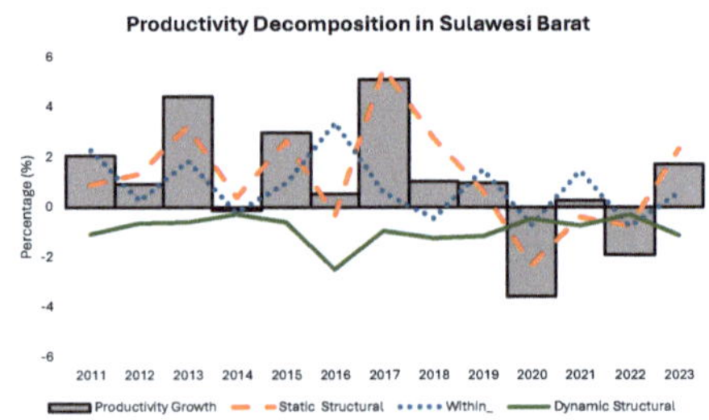
Productivity Decomposition in Sulawesi Barat
Percentage (%)
2011 2012 2013 2014 2015 2016 2017 2018 2019 2020 2021 2022 2023
Productivity Growth
Static Structural
Within_
Dynamic Structural

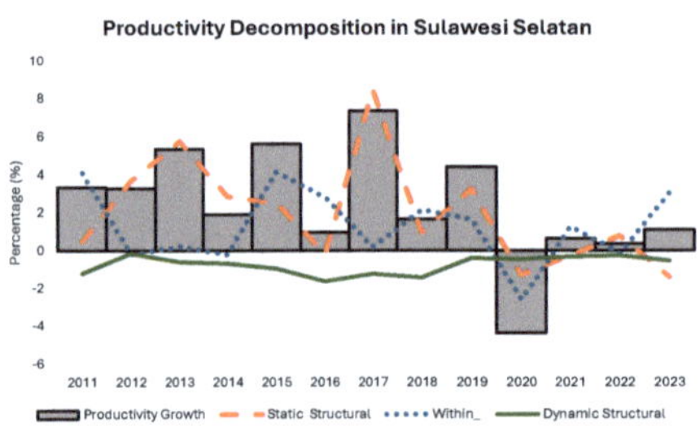
Productivity Decomposition in Sulawesi Selatan
Percentage (%)
2011 2012 2013 2014 2015 2016 2017 2018 2019 2020 2021 2022 2023
Productivity Growth
Static Structural
Within_
Dynamic Structural

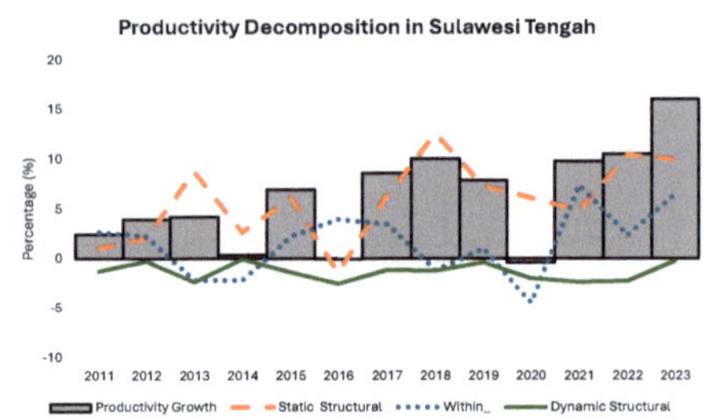
Productivity Decomposition in Sulawesi Tengah
Percentage (%)
2011 2012 2013 2014 2015 2016 2017 2018 2019 2020 2021 2022 2023
Productivity Growth
Static Structural
Within_
Dynamic Structural

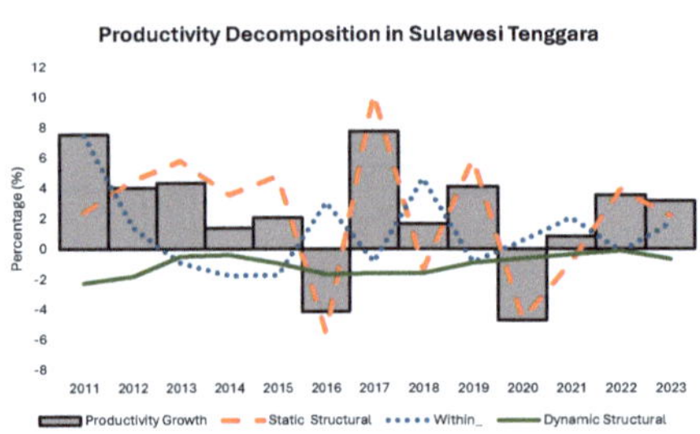
Productivity Decomposition in Sulawesi Tenggara
Percentage (%)
2011 2012 2013 2014 2015 2016 2017 2018 2019 2020 2021 2022 2023
Productivity Growth
Static Structural
Within_
Dynamic Structural

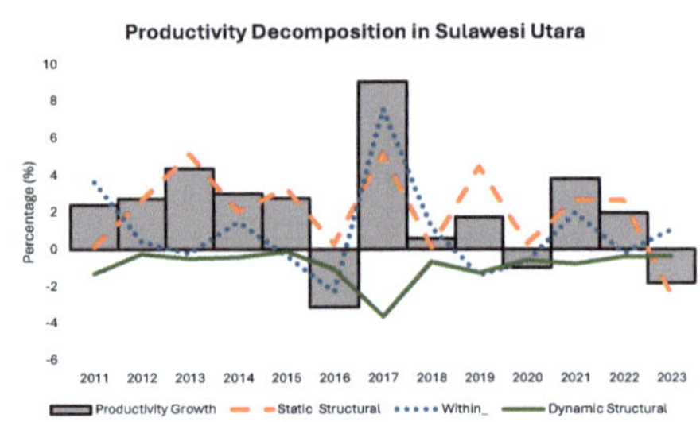
Productivity Decomposition in Sulawesi Utara
Percentage (%)
2011 2012 2013 2014 2015 2016 2017 2018 2019 2020 2021 2022 2023
Productivity Growth
Static Structural
Within_
Dynamic Structural

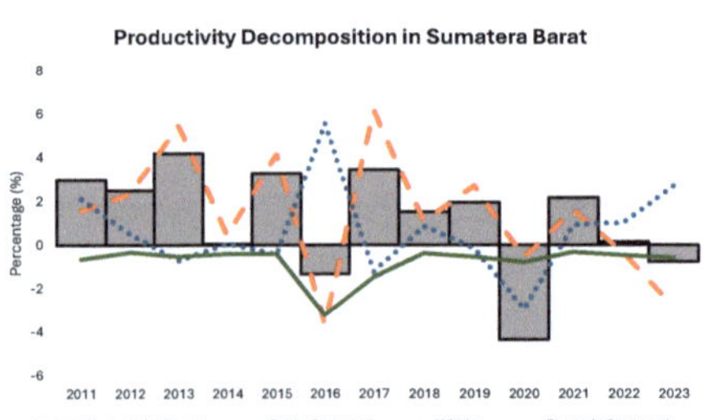
Productivity Decomposition in Sumatera Barat
Percentage (%)
2011 2012 2013 2014 2015 2016 2017 2018 2019 2020 2021 2022 2023
Productivity Growth
Static Structural
Within_
Dynamic Structural

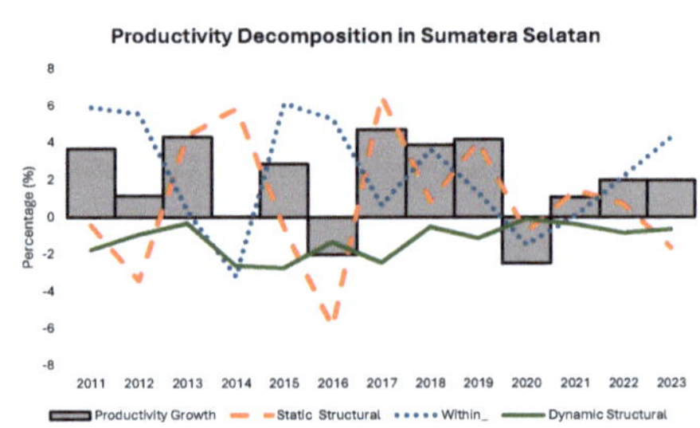
Productivity Decomposition in Sumatera Selatan
Percentage (%)
2011 2012 2013 2014 2015 2016 2017 2018 2019 2020 2021 2022 2023
Productivity Growth
Static Structural
Within_
Dynamic Structural

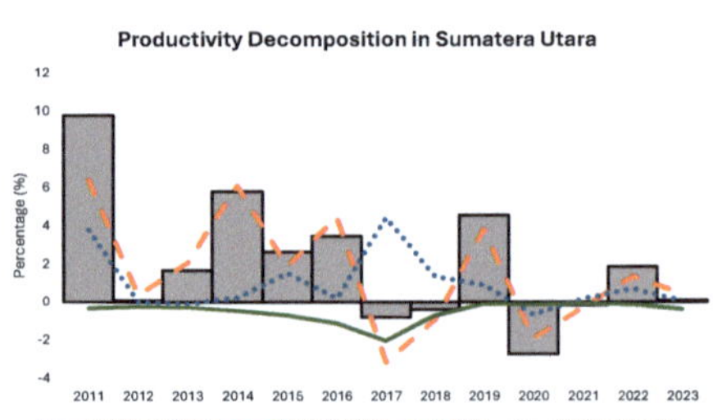
Productivity Decomposition in Sumatera Utara
Percentage (%)
2011 2012 2013 2014 2015 2016 2017 2018 2019 2020 2021 2022 2023
Productivity Growth
Static Structural
Within_
Dynamic Structural

Appendix 3.2: Changes in Sectoral Employment and Relative Productivity By Regions

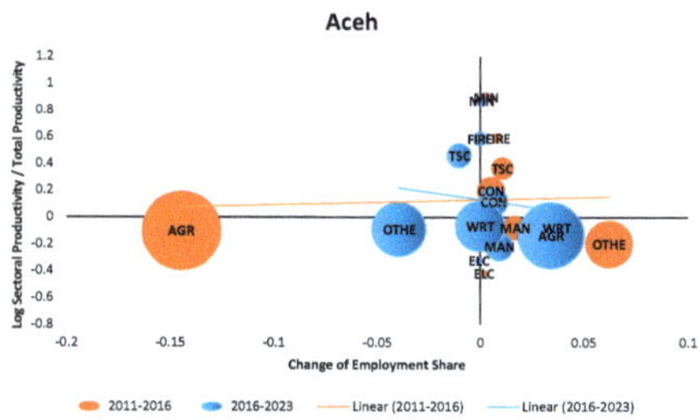

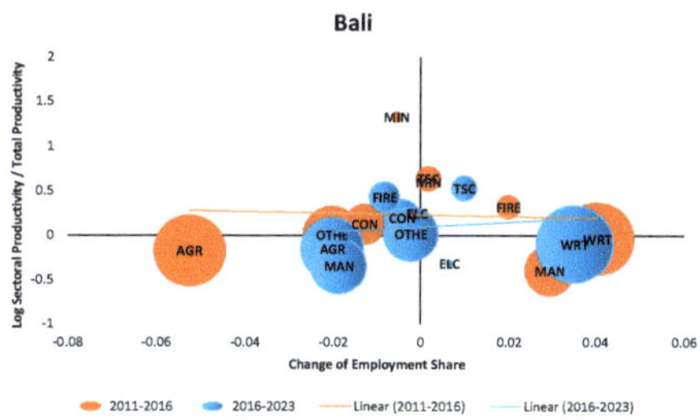

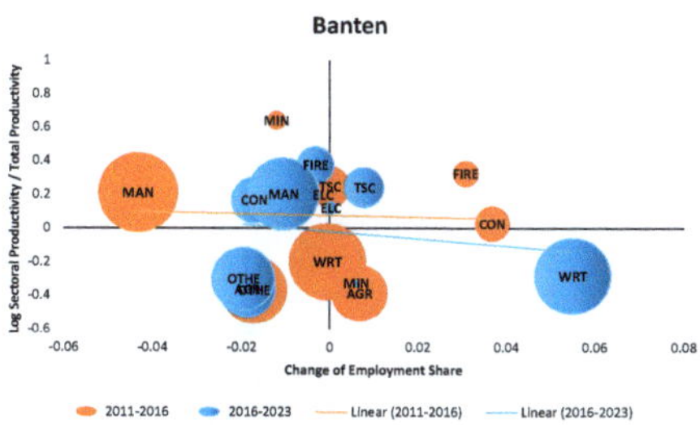

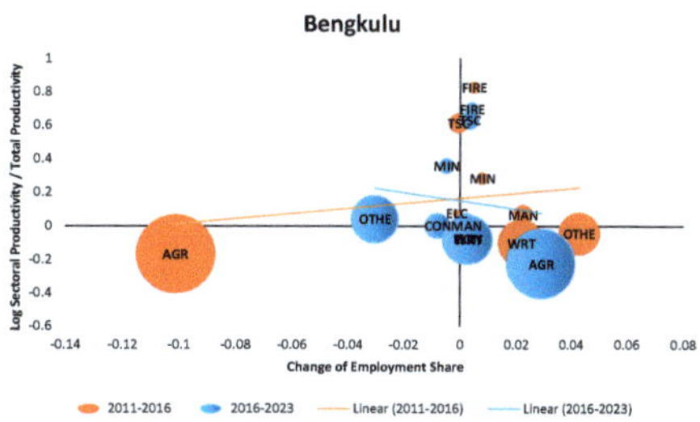

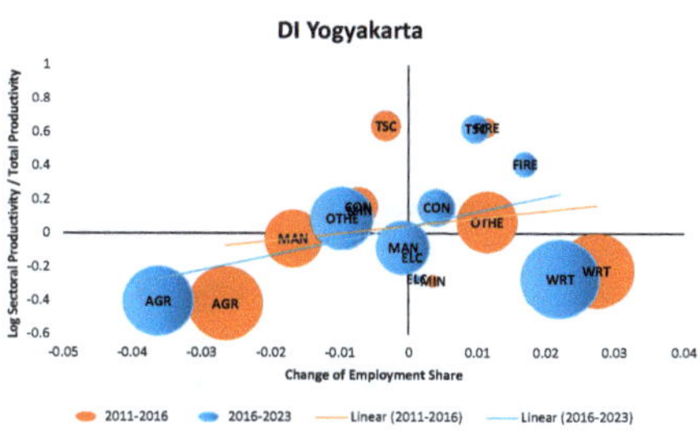

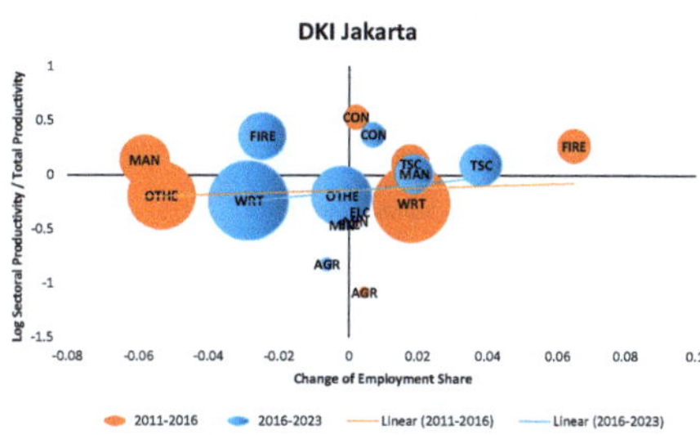

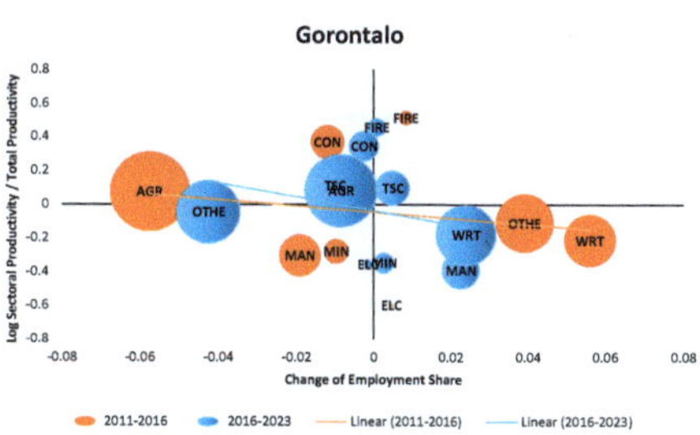

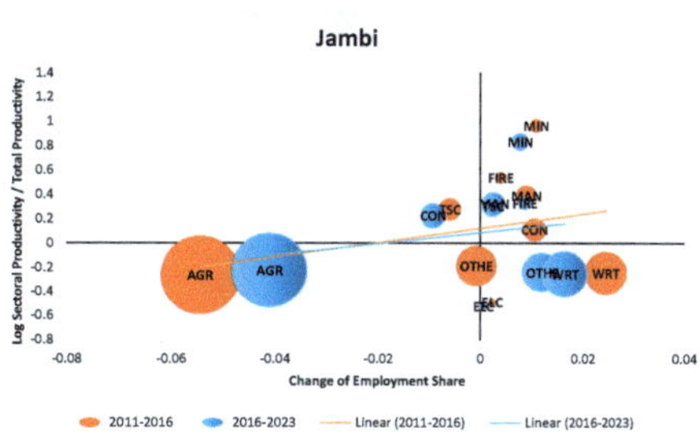

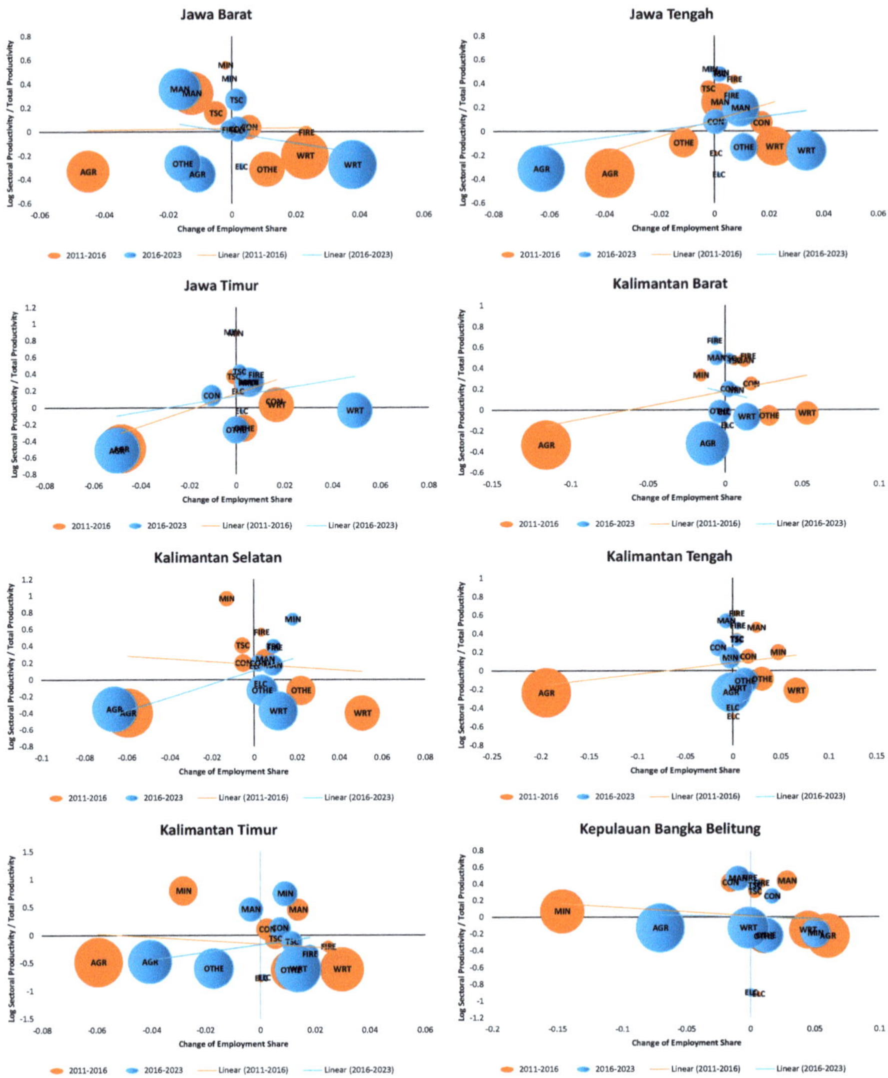
Jawa Barat
Jawa Tengah
Jawa Timur
Kalimantan Barat
Kalimantan Selatan
Kalimantan Tengah
Kalimantan Timur
Kepulauan Bangka Belitung
Log Sectoral Productivity / Total Productivity
Change of Employment Share
2011-2016
2016-2023
Linear (2011-2016)
Linear (2016-2023)

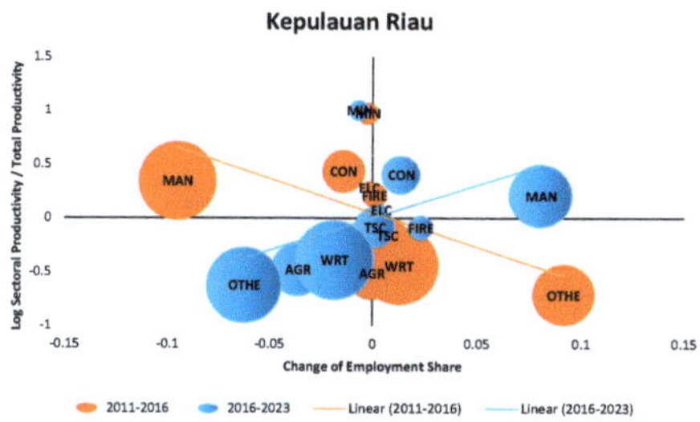
Kepulauan Riau
Log Sectoral Productivity / Total Productivity
Change of Employment Share
2011-2016
2016-2023
Linear (2011-2016)
Linear (2016-2023)

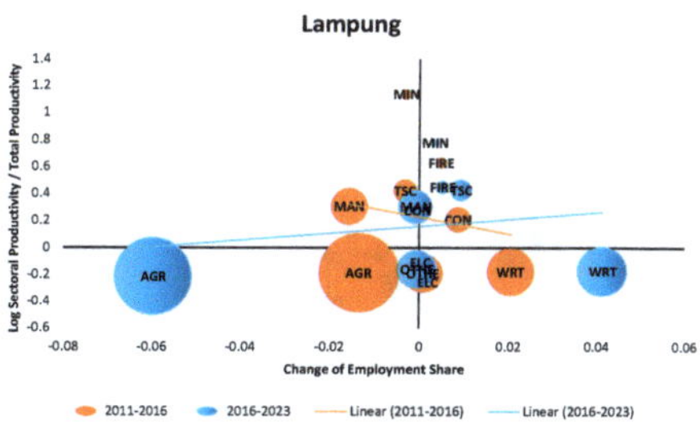
Lampung
Log Sectoral Productivity / Total Productivity
Change of Employment Share
2011-2016
2016-2023
Linear (2011-2016)
Linear (2016-2023)

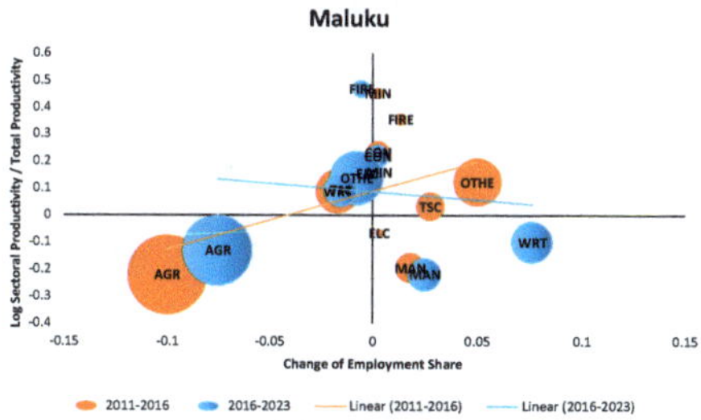
Maluku
Log Sectoral Productivity / Total Productivity
Change of Employment Share
2011-2016
2016-2023
Linear (2011-2016)
Linear (2016-2023)

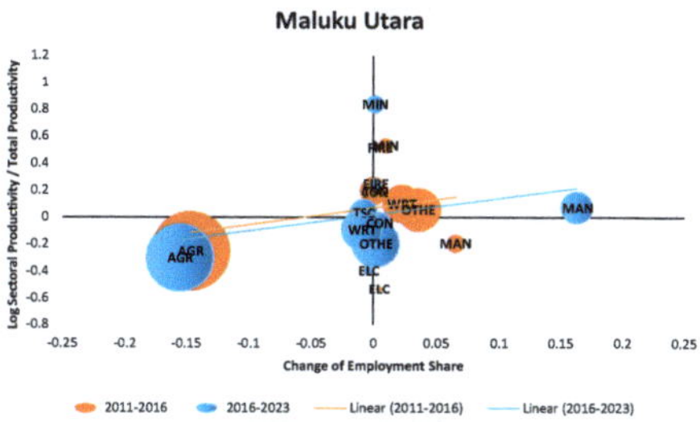
Maluku Utara
Log Sectoral Productivity / Total Productivity
Change of Employment Share
2011-2016
2016-2023
Linear (2011-2016)
Linear (2016-2023)

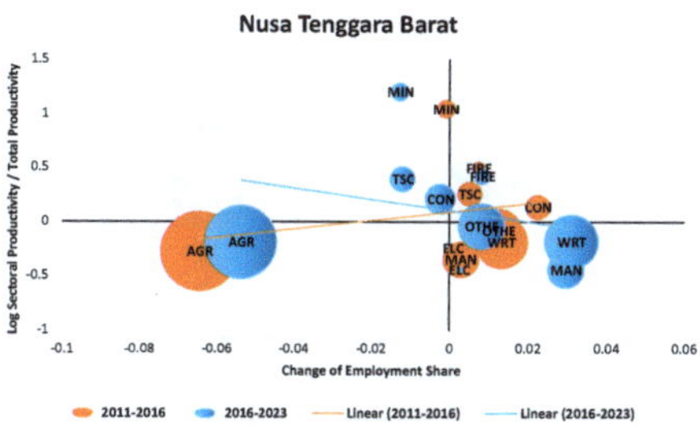
Nusa Tenggara Barat
Log Sectoral Productivity / Total Productivity
Change of Employment Share
2011-2016
2016-2023
Linear (2011-2016)
Linear (2016-2023)

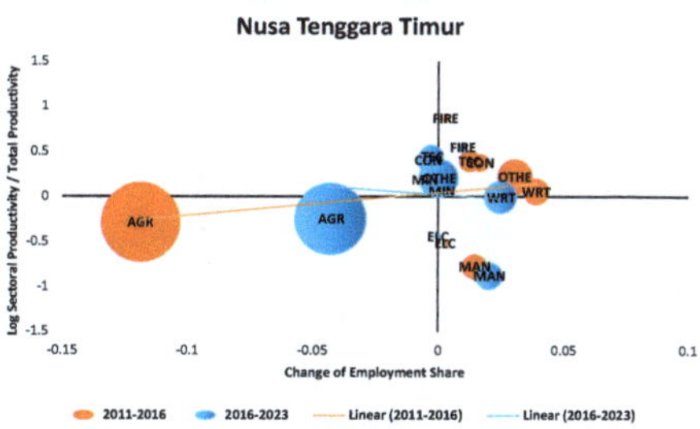
Nusa Tenggara Timur
Log Sectoral Productivity / Total Productivity
Change of Employment Share
2011-2016
2016-2023
Linear (2011-2016)
Linear (2016-2023)

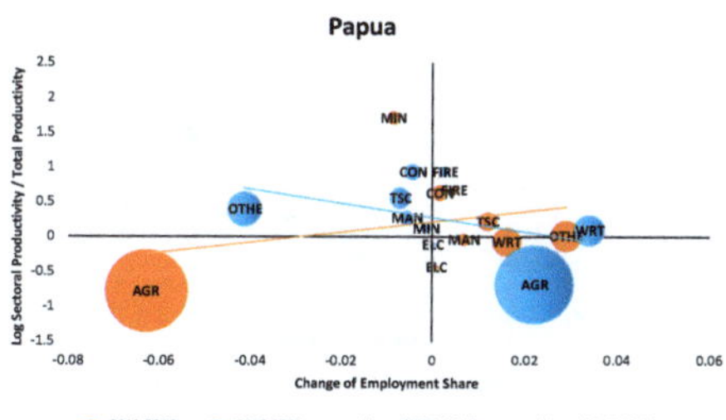
Papua
Log Sectoral Productivity / Total Productivity
Change of Employment Share
2011-2016
2016-2023
Linear (2011-2016)
Linear (2016-2023)

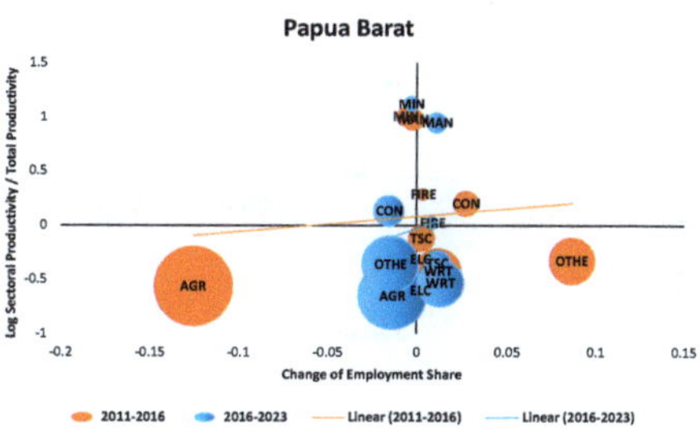
Papua Barat
Log Sectoral Productivity / Total Productivity
Change of Employment Share
2011-2016
2016-2023
Linear (2011-2016)
Linear (2016-2023)

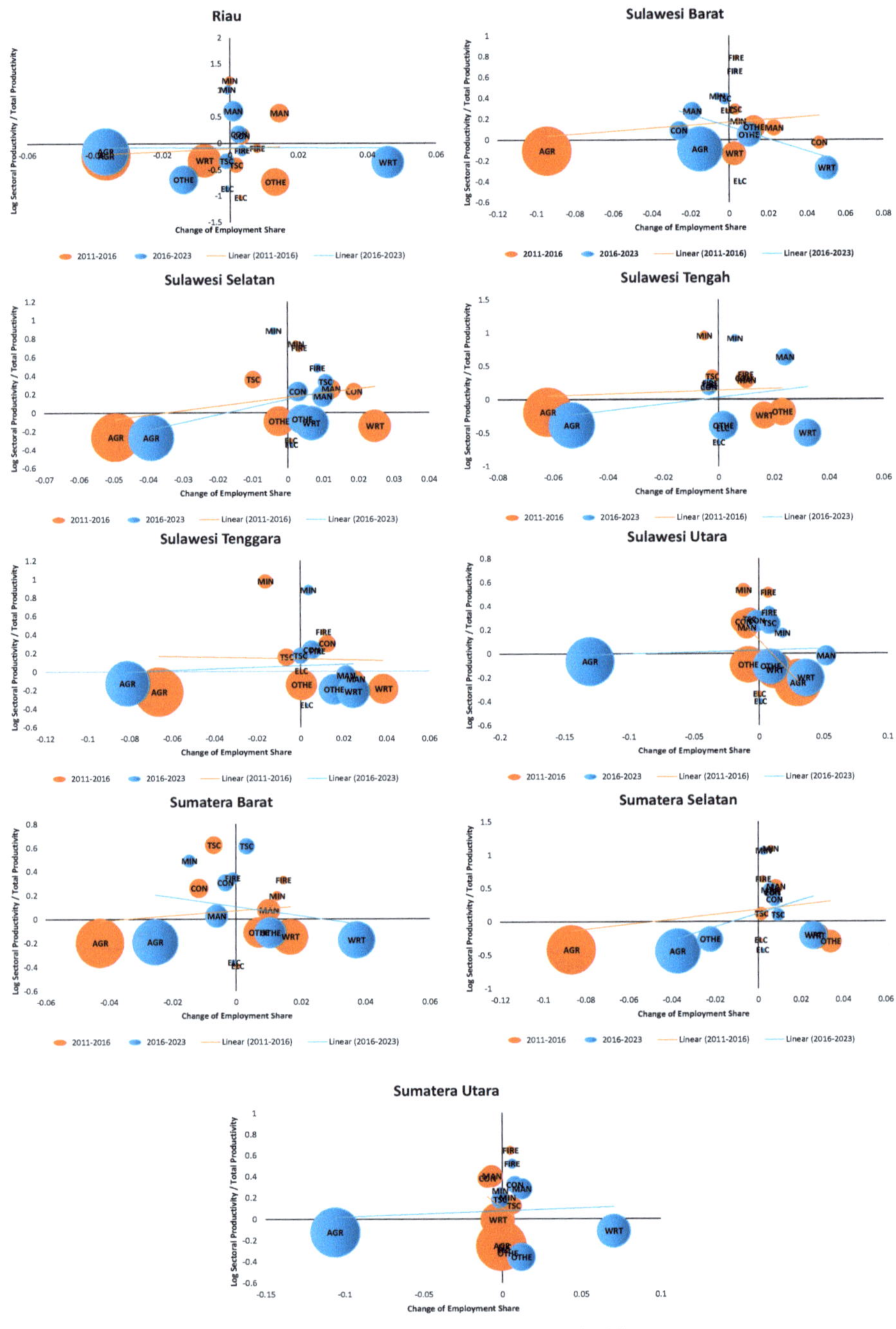
Riau
Log Sectoral Productivity / Total Productivity
Change of Employment Share
2011-2016
2016-2023
Linear (2011-2016)
Linear (2016-2023)
Sulawesi Barat
Sulawesi Selatan
Sulawesi Tengah
Sulawesi Tenggara
Sulawesi Utara
Sumatera Barat
Sumatera Selatan
Sumatera Utara

References

Azis, I. J. (2022). *Periphery and small ones matter: Interplay of policy and social capital*. Springer.

Azis, I. J. (2024). *Listen and design: On micro, small and medium enterprises*. Springer.

Gini, C. (1912). *Variabilità e Mutuabilità. Contributo allo Studio delle Distribuzioni e delle Relazioni Statistiche*. C. Cuppini.

Gini, C. (1921). Measurement of inequality of incomes. *Economic Journal, 31*(121), 124–126.

ILO. (2021). *ILO monitor: COVID-19 and the world of work* (8th edn.). Updated estimates and analysis.

Romer, P. M. (1990). Endogenous technological change. *Journal of Political Economy, 98*(5), S71–S102.

Chapter 4
Ignoring Spatial Factors

It was argued in Chap. 2 that any development process will involve centripetal-agglomeration forces. Left unattended, the development outcome would be tainted by growing inequality. In Chap. 3, the evidence was clearly shown that the inequality between regions in Indonesia is high by international standards and on the rise. This is despite the fact that various policies have been implemented to improve development outside of Jawa and eastern Indonesia. A fairly large amount of expenditure and investment was made and a substantial number of infrastructure had been built with the expectation that they would narrow the development gap between developed and less developed regions. Why did those policies not produce the intended outcome and why did the huge amount of built infrastructure fail to boost the economy and multipliers of less developed regions? Was the amount insufficient, or was it due to resource misallocation and mistargeted infrastructure?

There are two types of multipliers that we wish to use: intraregional multipliers and interregional multipliers. Both measure the effects of changes or shocks in the regional economy, but differ in focus and scope. Intraregional multipliers measure the direct and indirect economic impact within a single defined region, whereas interregional multipliers measure the economic impact between regions, tracking how economic changes in one region affect others, implying the presence of spillover effects across different regions due to direct trade, commuting, or supply chain links. When there is an injection or new spending in one region, say, infrastructure development, the money will circulate through various sectors by increasing the outputs of these sectors. Some of the outputs are produced locally, some in other regions. Hence, every time one sector in a region receives spending injection, additional incomes are generated in that region, as well as in other regions. In turn, this leads to further spending. 'Intraregional multipliers' operate when cascading effects occur within the region, 'interregional multipliers' work when the effects reach across regions.

I. J. Azis, *Monetary Whispers Across Space*,
https://doi.org/10.1007/978-981-95-4625-1_4

Before analyzing the working of both multipliers, we will first evaluate the degree of regional interdependence or integration within a region, as well as between regions, as it provides useful information about the extent of supply chains within and between regions. The discussions in this chapter begin with the evaluation of such regional and interregional interdependence before analyzing the reasons why large amount of investment in outside Jawa failed to reduce the interregional inequality by utilizing the intraregional and interregional multipliers.

4.1 Integration Within and Between Regions

A direct way to measure the degree of complex interrelations between sectors within a region is by using the coefficient of interdependence (COI) calculated from the input-output (IO) table of the region. To expose the role of spatial factors in determining the impact of investment or spending in one region on other regions, we calculate the COI using the interregional input output (IRIO) table.

Based on the four series of Indonesia's IRIO tables, Fig. 4.1 shows the degree of interdependence within Jawa, within non-Jawa, and between Jawa and non-Jawa. According to the size of COI, intersectoral interactions among sectors within both Jawa and non-Jawa have been fluctuating, declining during 2005–2010, increasing and decreasing in Jawa since then, and persistently increasing in non-Jawa. The interdependence between Jawa and non-Jawa also decreased from 2005 to 2010, then increased during 2010–2015, and slightly decreased in 2016. Using different

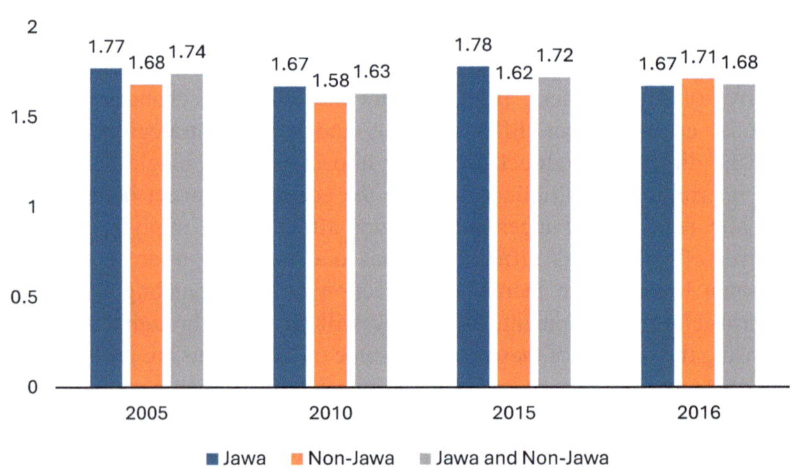

Fig. 4.1 Coefficient of Interdependence (COI): Jawa, Non-Jawa, National. *Source*: Author's calculation based on the IRIO tables

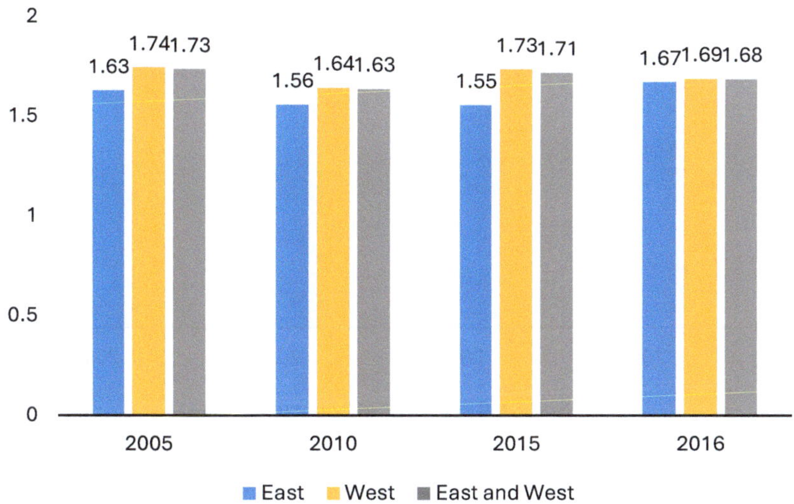

Fig. 4.2 Coefficient of Interdependence (COI): East, West, National. *Source*: Author's calculation based on the IRIO tables

regional classifications, that is, East and West, the interdependence within and between both regions fluctuated but decreased in recent years (Fig. 4.2).[1]

It is interesting to note that when we alter the coverage of West and East slightly, more specifically by re-shifting the Sulawesi position and put it into the West category, the COI between East and West became smaller, highlighting the notable role of Sulawesi in facilitating trade between Eastern and Western regions in Indonesia (Fig. 4.3).

With the recent opening of two new ports, the Soekarno-Hatta port and the Makassar new port in Sulawesi, it is likely that the already intensive trade between Sulawesi and other regions of eastern Indonesia will get higher. If Sulawesi is grouped with other regions in the West, the COI between West and East Indonesia will continue to increase and the COI within East Indonesia will decrease as logistics costs and residence time are expected to decrease.[2] Within Sulawesi itself, if the

[1] There is no clear scientific definition of East and West. Some use the Wallace Line (named after British naturalist Alfred Russel Wallace in the nineteenth century) as a reference. The imaginary line was drawn according to a stark difference in species on either side, and it runs through Indonesia between Borneo and Sulawesi, and Bali and Lombok, creating a biogeographical boundary dividing western Indonesia (Sundaland) with Asian-type flora and fauna (e.g. tigers, elephants, and rhinoceroses) and eastern Indonesia (Wallacea), which has a mix of Asian and Australasian species.

[2] Until now, the export of mainstay products from Sulawesi has been conducted through Tanjung Perak Port in Surabaya or Tanjung Priok Port in Jakarta. The lack of integration between the ports, industrial estates, and factories, had caused Indonesia's logistics costs high.

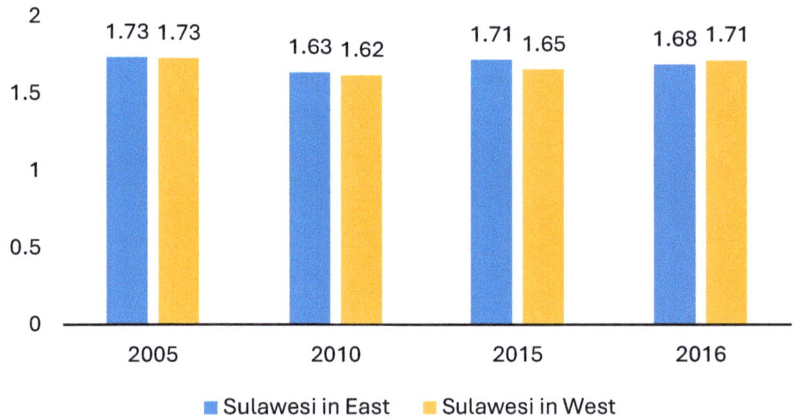

Fig. 4.3 Coefficient of Interdependence (COI): Between East & West. *Source*: Author's calculation based on the IRIO tables

support infrastructure is built to facilitate access from the production centers to these ports, growth could accelerate.

It is clear that except in 2016 Jawa's degree of integration is higher than in regions outside of Jawa, confirming the more developed regional status of Jawa.[3] Similarly, integration in West Indonesia is higher than in the eastern regions. It is also clear that COI is fairly sensitive to the regional classification used, and the role of Sulawesi has been quite prominent in facilitating the supply chain for the economy within Eastern Indonesia and between Western and Eastern regions.

4.2 Multipliers Asymmetry

Suppose that we have two sets of regions, developed and less developed ones, and we wish to narrow the development gap between the two. According to neoclassical economics, if no specific course of action is taken, the 'invisible hand' will eventually work to close the gap. Indeed, given the initial interregional inequality, the neo-classical model postulates that by allowing markets to work and letting capital free to move, a narrower gap between regions will eventually be reached. So long as the production functions in the regions are homogeneous of degree zero and capital is free to move, a convergence pattern will take place irrespective of the degree of flexibility in resource allocation–elasticity of substitution–within each region. However, how long it will take to reach the new equilibrium will depend on that elasticity. If we wish to speed up the process by being pro-active,

[3] Note that the IRIO for 2016 was not fully based on survey. Some of the data were estimated using a particular technique and assumptions. We are not too confident about the accuracy of that IRIO.

it seems logical that the best course of action is to allocate more resources to the less developed regions. More investment and subsidies are expected to increase the output and income of these regions. In the case of Indonesia, if we increase investment and build more infrastructure outside Jawa or Eastern Indonesia, over time the gap between Jawa and non-Jawa or Eastern Indonesia should be narrowed. Hence, the instinctive course of action to reduce the gap is to invest more outside Jawa, or, if we are patient enough to wait, to let markets work without interruption.

Such conclusions are based on the assumption that there are no centripetal or agglomeration forces at work, contrary to the specification of spatial economics. In spatial economics, the first part of the recommendation should be conditional, and the second part is unlikely to hold, and hence to be rejected. The proactive measure of simply investing in less developed regions can backfire, making the initial inequality worse. Part of the reason is because it undermines the nature of interactions between the two regions (centripetal or agglomeration forces), the existing institutions, and the prevailing social capital. If these factors are taken into account in the design of the policy, the type and location of investment matters critically. What kind of infrastructure will be built outside Jawa or eastern Indonesia and in which sectors investments are to be made are key questions that need to be addressed before formulating policy. The effectiveness of policy depends on it very much.

The challenge is how do we measure institutions and social capital? There are some direct and indirect indicators, as well as tangible and intangible indicators, that one can consider. Intangibles range from regulatory quality, government effectiveness, property right, trust, and network between communities and other stakeholders (social engagement/cohesion). Gauging the intensity of each of them can be done by conducting surveys, case studies, interviews, or focus group discussions involving stakeholders to ensure that deeper insights are obtained. Some approaches are qualitative in nature and only applicable to specific institutional frameworks, others combine quantitative and qualitative approaches with broader applications.[4] In essence, measuring the role of institutions and social capital involves evaluating their influence on specific goals (economic growth, productivity, or social well-being).

However, tangible factors cannot be dismissed. They are critical to influencing the effect of policies. The structure of the local economy, the level of development, and the local conditions with respect to transport and other infrastructure all play a significant role. Together with intangible factors, they jointly determine the outcomes and effects of policies through direct and indirect channels. Whatever the results and the observed indicators are, they reflect the result of the interplay between all these factors.

[4] An example of the latter is the analysis of MSME based on field surveys and questionnaires using the mechanism design theory (MDT), in which the role of network as one of the elements of social capital was highlighted (Azis, 2024).

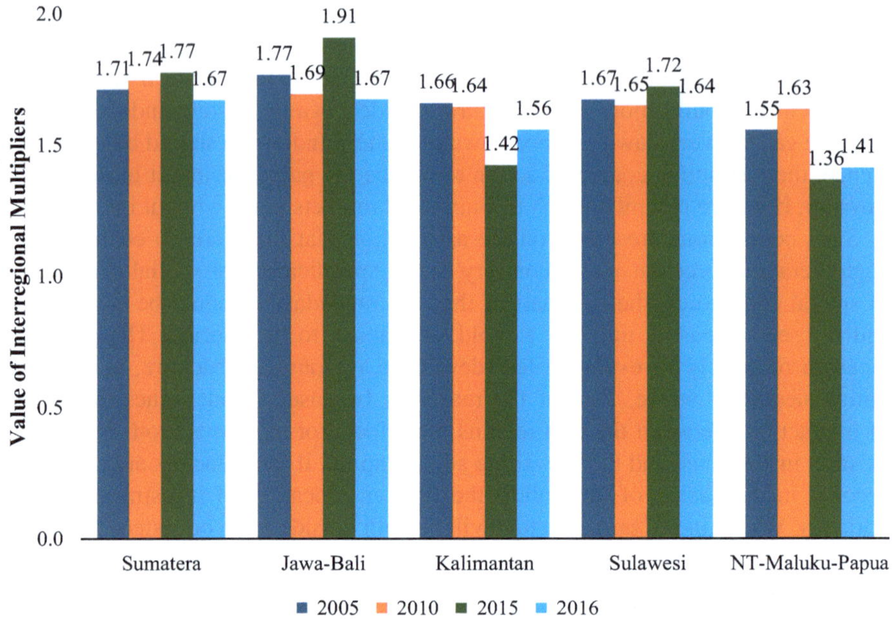

Fig. 4.4 Intraregional multipliers from a shock in construction sector. *Source*: Author's calculation based on IRIO Tables, 2005, 2010, 2015, and 2016

Without disentangling the contribution of each factor, we focus on particular outcome and observed indicator: intraregional multipliers and interregional multipliers. They basically measure how initial changes in an activity (e.g., putting new investment or building infrastructure) create ripple effects throughout the economy and cause amplification to the original impact within and across regions, respectively.

To delineate the ripple effects of the original spending, by using these two types of multipliers, we can make a comparison between the direct and indirect effects of a spending in one region to other regions, and the direct and indirect effects of a spending in a reverse direction. Hence, if a certain investment made in Jawa causes some amplified effects within Jawa (intraregional multiplier) and spillover effects outside Jawa (interregional multiplier), the latter will be compared with the spillover effects on Jawa of the same amount of investment made outside Jawa. The magnitude of those multipliers reflects the net result of the interplay between various tangible and intangible factors described above.

Figure 4.4 shows the intraregional multipliers and Fig. 4.5 shows the interregional multipliers caused by a shock (increased activities) in the construction sector related to infrastructure. Between the five regions listed, the highest intraregional multipliers were in Jawa and Sumatera and the lowest was in NT-Maluku-Papua (Eastern Indonesia). Over time, the trend indicates that these multipliers increased in the former and decreased in the latter. The differences in tangible and intangible factors mentioned above are the reasons behind such a trend.

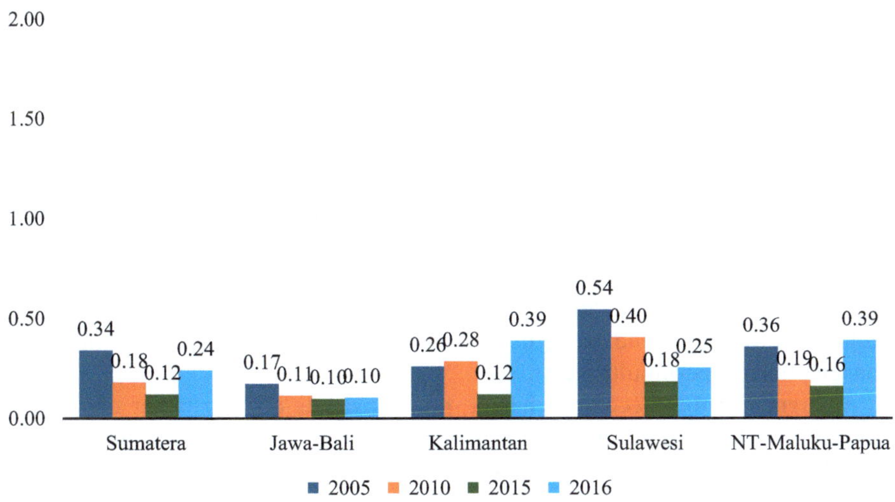

Fig. 4.5 Interregional multipliers from a shock in construction sector. *Source*: Author's calculation based on IRIO Tables, 2005, 2010, 2015, and 2016

In terms of inequality between regions, interregional multipliers are more relevant to evaluate. Figure 4.5 shows the interregional multipliers based on the backward linkage measure, in which the origin of the shock (construction sector) and the input-producing industries are not located in the same region.[5] Almost in a perfect contrast with the intraregional multipliers, the interregional multipliers outside Jawa were larger than in Jawa, implying that the economic gains of activities taking place outside Jawa received elsewhere (mostly Jawa) exceeded those of activities taking place in Jawa. The multipliers outside Jawa fluctuated and became larger in the last year of observation. In contrast, the multipliers in Jawa fell almost persistently. Hence, from the interregional multipliers perspective alone one could have predicted that the evidence in Indonesia was not in line with what the neo-classical theory suggests. The sign of convergence was absent. A combination of differences in regional economic structure and the prevailing institutions between Jawa and non-Jawa contributed to this trend.

Another notable contrast is in the regional distribution of multipliers. Although Jawa and Sumatera had the largest intraregional multipliers, almost the opposite occurred in the interregional multipliers, where those outside Jawa exceeded the multipliers in Jawa and Sumatera. Any infrastructure development taking place in eastern Indonesia (NT-Maluku-Papua) generated much higher multipliers throughout the rest of the country compared to the multipliers generated if the infrastructure

[5] Backward linkage refers to the intensity of connections that a particular sector has with its suppliers or the input-providing industries. In the interregional context, it basically measures the spillovers of activities in the origin sector and region to upstream activities in other regions.

was built in Jawa. As shown in the figure, the difference reached as much as four times larger during the last year of observation (0.39 versus 0.10).

Both the intra- and interregional multipliers described above are still underestimated because they exclude the role of increased consumption. When a particular sector in a region receives spillover effects from activities outside the region, not only the production of the region that will increase, consumption will also increase, and the increased consumption generates another round of direct and indirect effects. Hence, we need to include those effects in the intersectoral multipliers through which the increase in consumption leads to greater demand for sectoral outputs. This is known as "induced effects", and the multipliers are called Type-II multipliers, which should be higher than those that exclude the role of increased consumption (Type-I multipliers).

As argued in the preceding chapter, productivity is a much better measure to gauge the welfare and development outcome. Suppose we wish to find the impact of 1000 IDR increased productivity in the construction sector in Jawa. Based on Type-I multipliers, the productivity in Jawa will increase by 1765 IDR and in non-Java it is 171 IDR, or only 10% of Jawa's gains (Fig. 4.6a). However, if we include the induced effect from increased consumption, the gains would be higher. The national average of total increase is 432 IDR, and the increase of labor productivity in Jawa and non-Jawa is 2284 IDR and 407 IDR, respectively (Fig. 4.6b). That is, Jawa's gains are about 5.6 times larger than non-Jawa's gains.

If the same amount of increased productivity occurs outside Jawa, the increase in per labor output outside Jawa based on Type I multipliers will be 1740 IDR, while in Java 282 IDR , or about 16% of Non-Jawa's gains (Fig. 4.7a). But if we use Type II multipliers, the increase will be 1958 IDR and 763 IDR, respectively, and the national productivity will increase by 401 IDR (Fig. 4.7b). That is, non-Jawa gains will be 2.6 times larger than Jawa gains. Hence, apart from the fact that Type II multipliers obviously generate greater total gains, given the prevailing structure of the economy of both regions and the interregional relationship between them, any increase in construction activity will generate greater national gains and a better interregional distribution if it is done in Jawa than outside Jawa. Again, similar to the results of the previous evaluation, under current conditions, if the course of action is simply investing more in outside Jawa, the outcome will worsen rather than improve the interregional inequality. The centripetal or agglomeration forces are too strong to counter and the end result is ironically the opposite of what was originally intended.

To further dive into the issue, it is of interest to find out in which regions outside Jawa the increased activities will generate the largest gains to Jawa. Also of interest is the other-way round question: Which regions outside of Jawa received the largest economic gains from increased activities in Jawa? Figures 4.8 and 4.9 show the difference between the interregional multipliers generated by increased activities in Non-Jawa versus those in Jawa. In 2005, any increase in activities in Sumatera generated around 0.16 multiplier to Jawa-Bali, while the opposite direction (from Jawa to Sumatera) generated only less than 0.04. That is almost 40 times larger. Although the trend shows a fluctuation, the size of interregional

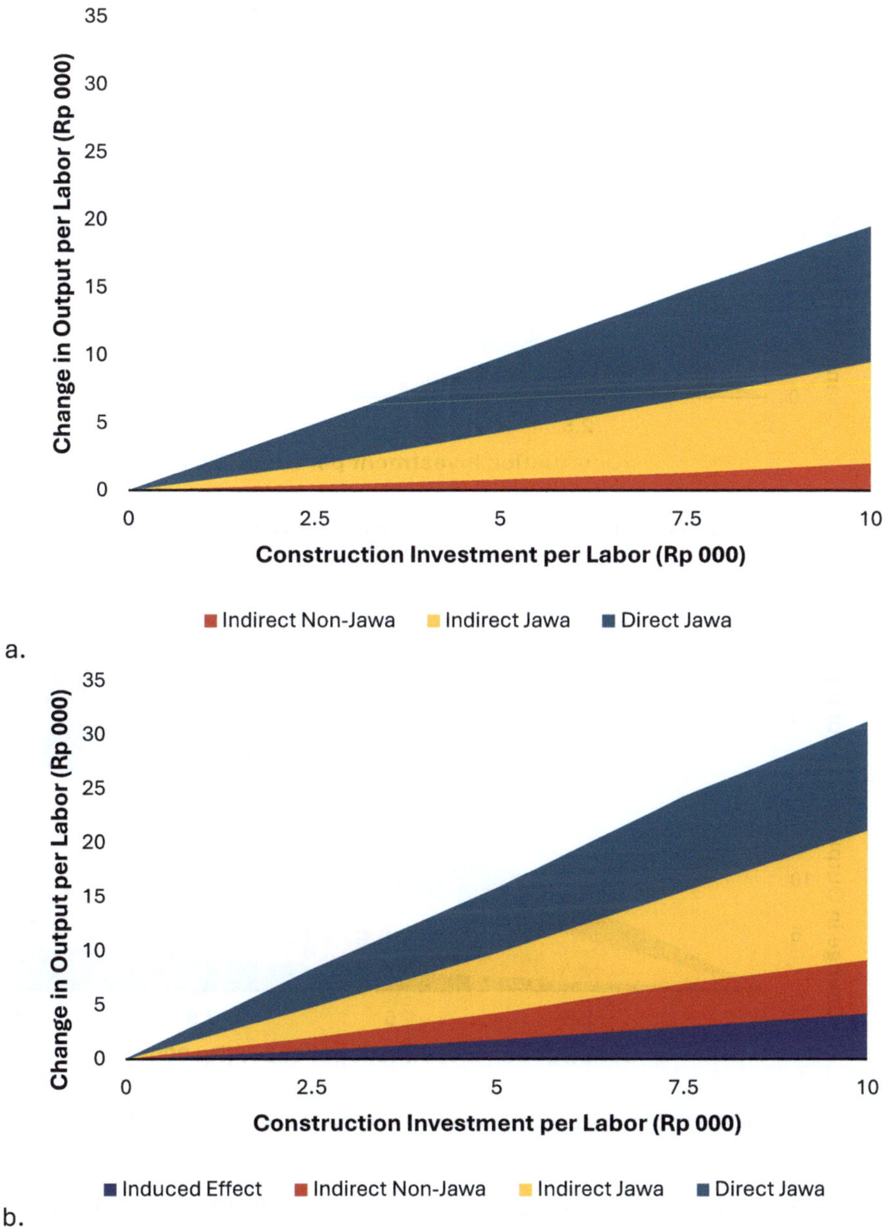

Fig. 4.6 Regional and national productivity change due to: (**a**) 1000 IDR productivity increase in Jawa construction (Type-I multipliers). (**b**) 1000 IDR productivity increase in Jawa final demand (Type-II multipliers). *Source*: Author's calculation based on IRIO

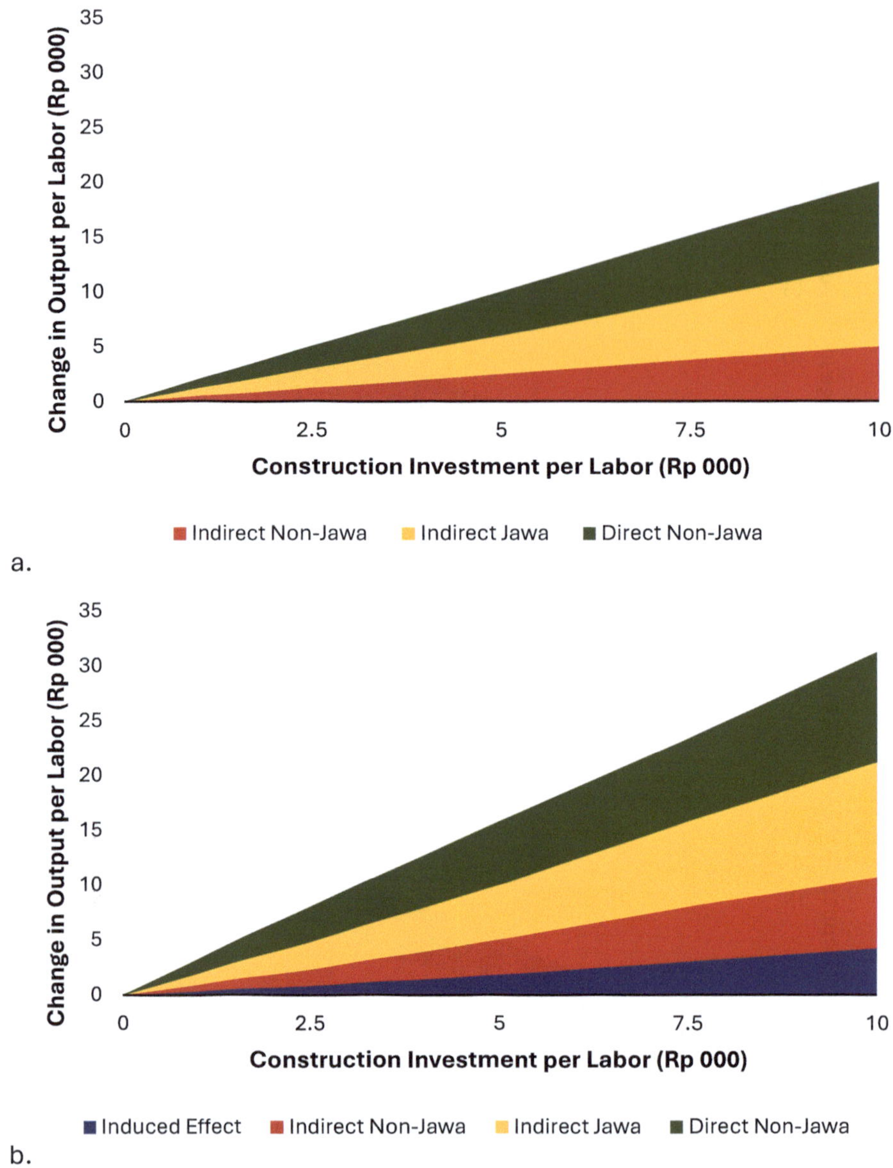

Fig. 4.7 Regional and national productivity change due to: (**a**) 1000 IDR productivity increase in non-Jawa (**b**) 1000 IDR productivity increase in non-Jawa final demand (Type-II multipliers). *Source:* Author's calculation based on IRIO

Fig. 4.8 Interregional multipliers from non-Jawa to Jawa: Backward linkages. *Source*: Author's calculation based on IRIO Tables, 2005, 2010, 2015, and 2016

multipliers from all regions outside Jawa to Jawa increased simultaneously in the last year of observation, the largest being the multipliers from the Eastern Indonesia regions.

More importantly, it is noticeable that the size of the interregional multipliers from Jawa to all regions outside of Jawa was much smaller than that generated in the opposite direction (asymmetric pattern). This is another evidence showing that efforts to narrow the development gap between Jawa and non-Jawa cannot be done by simply making more investment or building more infrastructure in outside Jawa. The centripetal forces combined with tangible and intangible factors outside of Jawa will cause some of the benefits of the development of the infrastructure brought into Jawa through various mechanisms.[6]

Note that the multipliers shown in Fig. 4.9 are Type-I multipliers. The asymmetry of gains between regions is actually more intense than what is shown in that figure.

[6] The interregional multipliers are based on the backward linkages measure. A similar asymmetric pattern is also detected in interregional multipliers based on forward linkages (available upon request). Essentially, forward links are the key to expanding economic activities by leveraging the output of one industry in a region to develop and grow others within and outside the regions. Such links can apply to job creation, ideas and innovation, and other benefits beyond output production.

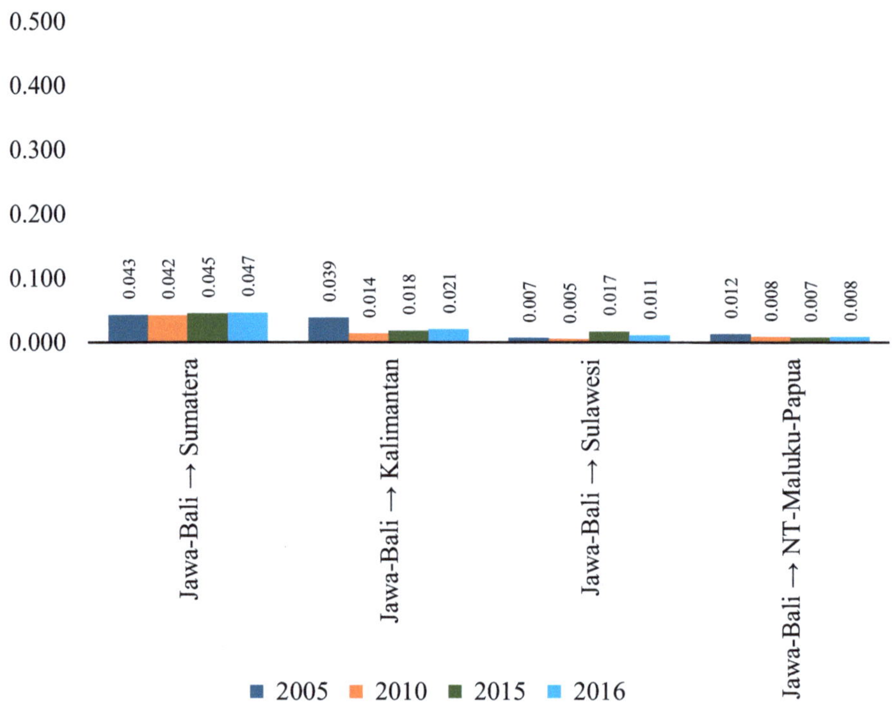

Fig. 4.9 Interregional multipliers from Jawa to non-Jawa: Backward linkages. *Source*: Author's calculation based on IRIO Tables, 2005, 2010, 2015, and 2016

Induced by spillovers from increased activities outside Jawa, the income level in Jawa increases, and that stimulates higher consumption spending too. In turn, the increased consumption adds more demand for both local and non-local products. As the cycle continues, the Type-II multiplier kicks in and is larger than the Type-I multiplier. In addition, different consumption elasticity in each sector amplifies the size of multiplier further.[7] Figure 4.10 shows the varying size of multipliers of different types: Type I and Type II multipliers without elasticity adjustment, and Type II multipliers with elasticity adjustment. Notice that the difference between Type I and Type II multipliers without elasticity adjustment is already substantial. When an adjustment in consumption elasticity is included, the difference is more striking.

For example, the difference between the Type I and Type II interregional multipliers of increased activities in Sumatera with spillovers to Jawa was more than nine times (1.212 versus 0.133). For Type II multipliers without elasticity adjustment the difference is 3.72 times, and with elasticity adjustment it is 3.92

[7] In social accounting matrix (SAM), the multipliers that ignore different elasticity is called Accounting Multipliers, and the one that takes into account the differences in elasticity is known as Fixed Price Multipliers.

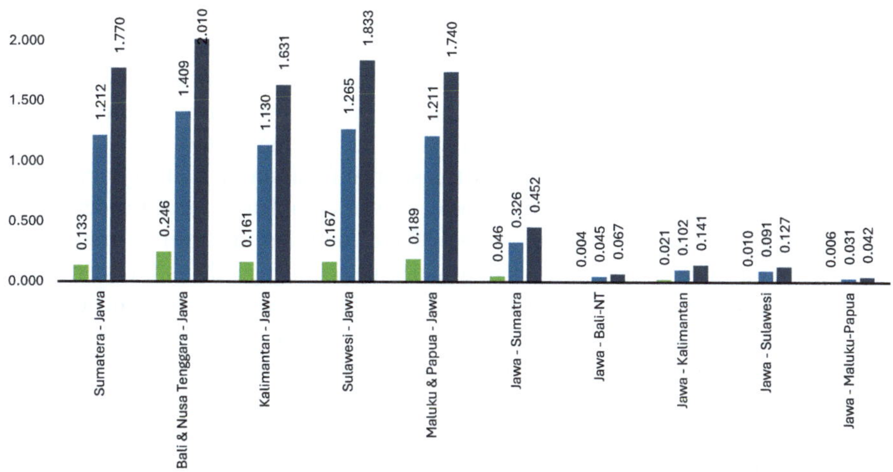

Fig. 4.10 Interregional multipliers: Type-II and type-I. *Source*: Author's calculation based on 2016 IRIO Table

times. Both are greater than the difference for the Type-I multiplier discussed earlier. If the increased activities are in other non-Jawa regions, the difference was much larger than the results from the previous Type-I multipliers.

More importantly, the multiplier asymmetry between spillovers of activities outside Jawa to Jawa versus spillovers of activities outside Jawa to outside Jawa was also striking. For Sumatera-Jawa pair, Bali & NT-Jawa pair, Kalimantan-Jawa pair, Sulawesi-Jawa pair, and Maluku & Papua-Jawa pair the differences were, respectively, 3.72 times, 31.3 times, 11.1 times, 13.9 times and 39.1 times. Those are the comparisons for Type II multipliers without elasticity adjustment. When adjustment is included, the differences were greater: 3.9 times, 30 times, 11.6 times, 14.4 times, and 41.4 times. Hence, the spillover benefits received by Jawa from increased activities in eastern Indonesia were the highest, much larger than the spillover benefits received by eastern Indonesia from increased activities in Jawa.

The above observation shows that the use of Type-II multiplier clearly reinforces the earlier conclusions from the case of using the Type-I multiplier. From policy perspectives, without addressing the structure, institutions, and prevailing social capital of the region, the more investment or infrastructure development carried out in eastern Indonesia, the greater the benefits Jawa will receive. Any increase in output and income generated by investment in eastern Indonesia is counterbalanced by greater spillovers benefiting Jawa. Simply pouring more money into Eastern Indonesia (or any regions outside Jawa for that matter) will not guarantee that the gap between Jawa and non-Jawa will be reduced. In the worst case, it could backfire by making the gap wider.

Building infrastructure not aligned with local needs is not only ineffective, but it can have several negative impacts as well, ranging from wasted and depleted resources, under-utilization that leads to inefficiency, missed opportunities for more impactful investments (high opportunity costs), unfulfilled potentials if it cuts through valuable site such as protected forest or fertile land, destroyed ecosystem when it causes pollution, and social conflict when it disrupts the livelihood of local businesses, farmers, and communities. In general, misaligned infrastructure creates obstacles instead of opportunities and can become a long-term liability for the region. As the tide rises, the currents will pull it back to the depths.

Take the case of the development of transport infrastructure such as port (air or sea) and road construction. After the project was completed, local residents and the business community took advantage of the facilities to travel or trade their products in Jawa. The ease of traveling and transporting goods as a result of the new infrastructure reinforced Jawa's attraction. Some of the businesses outside Jawa may eventually decide to move to Jawa, and some may keep the operations locally, but conduct the transactions with parties in Jawa, that is, purchase more goods from Jawa or sell and ship their products to Jawa. The built infrastructure reinforced this practice. In either way, centripetal forces reigned. During our field studies, we found that many local businesses did exactly that after the completion of ports or road infrastructure.

A notable example is packaging activity. Many small and medium enterprises (SMEs) outside Jawa had to send their products to Jawa to be packaged in, or buy packaging materials from, Jawa, since there were virtually no packaging industries available locally. Even with a new or improved infrastructure, the cost of shipping was too expensive for them, making it difficult for businesses to improve their efficiency. One of our respondents who runs a coffee business outside of Jawa expressed his frustration about this. The new infrastructure, which was costly to build and renovate, did not reduce transport costs. In the end, he decided to move a large part of his business operations to Jawa. Another evidence of centripetal forces at work.

Upon further exploration of the issue, it turns out that the new transport infrastructure helped only to reduce the time required to ship goods, but at higher costs. Since many businesses relied on the packaging industries in Jawa, they faced basically the same problem, preventing them from being more competitive. According to local bankers and members of the business community whom we interviewed, the completion of road construction and airport renovation was paradoxically seen as an opportunity to do business in Jawa, rather than stimulating local industries or strengthening existing ones. In the reverse case, very few businesses outside the region were attracted to do business in the region.

This pattern is widespread in regions outside Jawa, albeit to varying degrees. Yet, building infrastructure is very costly. If no other supporting policies are put in place and the existing trend continues, it is likely that many infrastructure projects outside Jawa will make the gap between Jawa and non-Jawa growing, rather than narrowing. New businesses will move to Jawa, while more local resources from outside Jawa are pulled towards Jawa (trickle-up phenomenon).

Many businesses in less developed regions are traditional in nature and operate using simple tools and technology. The largest share is in trade activities, especially retail trade, with low productivity and small in size. In terms of the number of establishments and workers, they are the largest in the region. It is a common practice for these businesses to purchase goods outside the regions, mainly Jawa, and sell them locally. They earn enough profit margin by doing so.

Putting money to finance infrastructure development into such an economic structure could be wasteful if the type of infrastructure is not aligned with the real need of those small businesses. Worse, since the built infrastructure has made it easier for them to purchase goods and ship to outside the region, there are no incentives for local businesses to purchase local products, even if such products are available or produced locally. The demand for local goods is very limited, which also means that there are no incentives for local producers and manufacturers to expand. On the other hand, the production of goods in developed regions is increased by the increase in demand from less developed regions. As a result, the development gap between regions grows wider.

Was the decision to invest or build infrastructure in less developed regions wrong? Absolutely not. These regions clearly need more investment. But the real question is what kind of investment or what type of infrastructure is to be built. This is where institutions and the prevailing social capital should be taken more seriously. Ignoring these factors makes the infrastructure ineffective. Many evidences have shown that projects and infrastructure development in some regions throughout Indonesia are not effective in stimulating the local economy and improving the welfare of local people. These projects are not what local people and business communities need.

Some of the projects do not only fail to improve people's living conditions but also worsen the standard of living due to environmental damage and social disruptions caused by the projects. In the end, for many of these regions, the infrastructure can be more of a liability than an asset.

References

Azis, I. J. (2024). *Listen and design: On micro, small and medium enterprises*. Springer.

Chapter 5
Broken Ladder: Was Monetary Policy Effective?

The main goal of monetary policy is to achieve economic stability and growth with certain targets to meet using a variety of monetary tools. Price stability is the most conventional goal where the target is to keep inflation at a certain level or within a specified range. The purpose is to protect the purchasing power of money and to enable businesses to make plans with more certainty. Related to price stability is exchange rate stability, because high inflation can be triggered by currency instability. Having a stable exchange rate allows monetary authority to better control inflation and achieve other macroeconomic goals using monetary tools such as interest rates. The stability of the price and exchange rate also helps maintain the social stability and cohesion needed for business and economic activities to operate without disruptions or disturbances due to unrest.

Through a dual mandate, central banks include employment as their target because what happens in the labor market could significantly impact economic stability and people's standard of living. Thus, monetary policy supports overall economic growth that increases employment. High unemployment not only causes social instability, but can also weaken growth, because a large portion of the population cannot contribute to the economy.

The challenge of achieving all these targets involves trade-offs. It requires careful balancing acts when choosing the combination of policy tools. Central banks can also use their ability to deliver information and policy statements to signal their intentions to the market. It is often the case that the trend of inflation is shaped by inflation expectations. Effective communication can help set such expectations.

Adding to the complexity is the addition of an emerging mandate concerning financial stability amid an increasing frequency of financial crisis. It becomes clear that financial markets are highly interconnected. Instability in one market could spread rapidly, affecting the functioning of other markets and the economy, leading to a broader economic crisis. The new goal of central banks is therefore to maintain financial stability. Just when the existing trade-offs seemed overwhelming, this

I. J. Azis, *Monetary Whispers Across Space*,
https://doi.org/10.1007/978-981-95-4625-1_5

additional mandate is coming into focus especially after the onset of the 2008 global financial crisis.

An additional mandate requires additional tools. This is where 'macroprudential' policies enter the policy framework. They are used to build resilience in the financial system and to mitigate systemic risks. Even during the non-crisis period, central banks have already enormous tasks as they face a more complex landscape. When monetary policies are designed to complement macroprudential policies, the working of monetary policies could be potentially disrupted. Unstable prices that undermine monetary policy can create unstable financial conditions. However, the latter can undermine monetary policy, making it harder to achieve price stability or promote economic growth. Central banks must walk a fine line to find the middle ground.

But monetary policy is not only about finding the right combination of policy tools. Examining the effectiveness of these tools is also important. Hence, it is imperative to ask was monetary policy effective thus far and, if not fully effective, what were the reasons for it? In the context of the theme of this book, it is our proposition that interregional inequality is one of the reasons that could hinder policy effectiveness. Our hypothesis is as follows: the greater the inequality between regions, the less effective the monetary policy becomes. Narrowing the development gap between high-income and low-income regions could improve the effectiveness of monetary policy.

In the next Section, we first take inventory of evidence on the three key variables of the central bank compared to the set targets in Indonesia. To test our hypothesis, we subsequently perform a preliminary analysis to determine whether there exists a relationship between interregional inequality and the effectiveness of monetary policy. In the last Section, we develop a model to look deeper into the significance of causality between the two.

5.1 Taking Inventory

Looking at three important goals of Bank Indonesia (inflation, exchange rate, and economic growth), we examine how close the actual values of these variables are to the targets. Judging by the differences between the actual inflation and the targets, Fig. 5.1 shows that since 2010 the actual inflation was not always in line with the targets. Especially during several quarters of the 'taper tantrum' period (since around 2013) when the world's commodity prices increased. During the early years of the COVID pandemic, inflation was also above targets, fluctuated, albeit on a declining trend. By smoothing out random fluctuations and noise, the moving average is used to reveal underlying trends and patterns that might otherwise be obscured by short-term variability. Using this metric, the gap between inflation and the targets was more obvious.

In the case of the exchange rate, the gap was not as large (Fig. 5.2). Unlike in the inflation story, the moving average of the exchange rate was generally lower

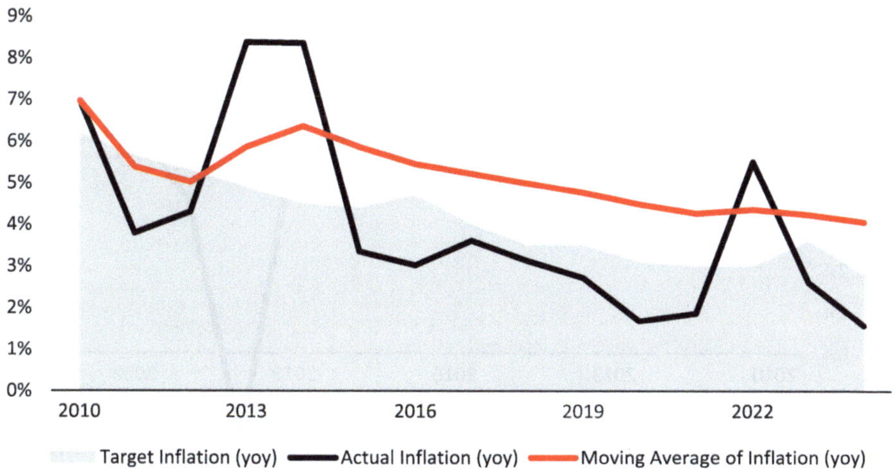

Fig. 5.1 Inflation rates: actual, moving average, and targets. *Source*: Bank Indonesia, BPS, and Ministry of Finance

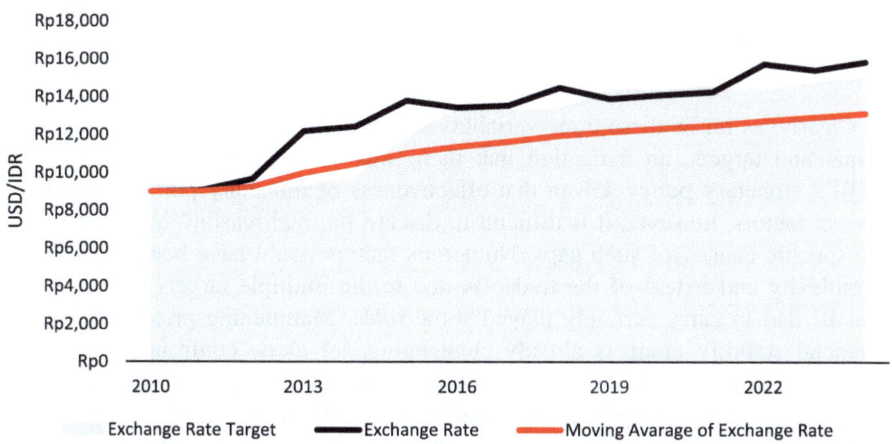

Fig. 5.2 Exchange rates: actual, moving average, and targets. *Source*: Bank Indonesia, BPS, and Ministry of Finance

(Rupiah was stronger) than the targets except around the time of the "taper tantrum," in which the actual rate was frequently higher (Rupiah was weaker) than the targets. The trend line also implies a weakening of the Rupiah.

The GDP growth shows a decelerating trend from around 6 to 5% range, closely following the targets (Fig. 5.3). However, during the period of observation, the actual rate was always lower than the target; only in one quarter of 2022 the actual rate was a little above the target. The y-o-y moving average was generally lower than the actual growth rate, except in 2016–2019.

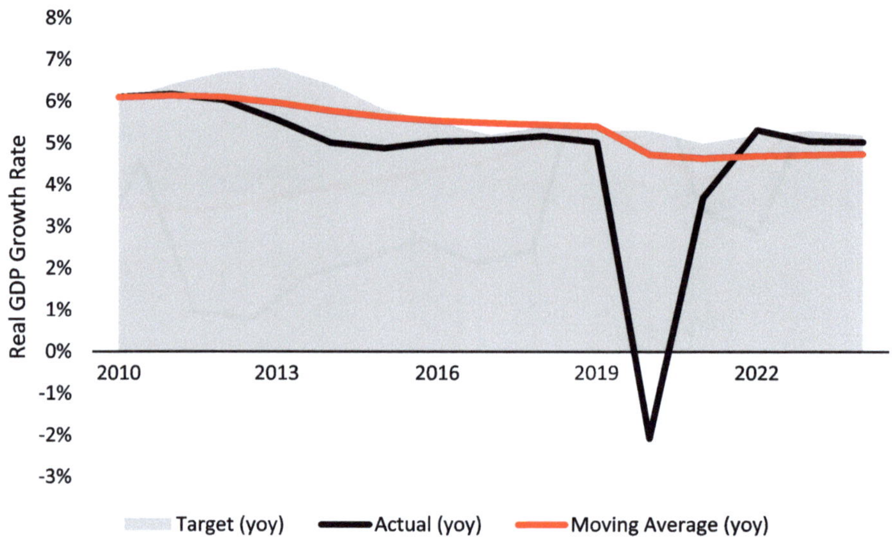

Fig. 5.3 GDP growth: actual, moving average, and targets. *Source*: Bank Indonesia, BPS, and Ministry of Finance

Clearly, as far as these three variables are concerned, there were gaps between actual and targets, an indication that there was some degree of ineffectiveness in BI's monetary policy. Given that effectiveness of monetary policy depends on several factors, however, it is difficult to discern the real reasons–let alone isolate the specific causes–of such gaps. Numerous factors could have been at play. The complexity and extent of the tradeoffs due to the multiple targets and mandates that BI had to carry certainly played some roles. Maintaining price stability and financial stability alone is already challenging, let alone confronting trade-offs between maximizing growth and combating inflation. The gap could also have been caused by persistent supply factors (weather, special holidays, supply chain, subsidy policy) and global factors (exchange rate movements, commodity prices, or foreign policy). All of these put a limit on the ability of the BI to control inflation.

To have a more accurate picture about the effectiveness of policy, we need to place the analysis in the context of domestic policy constraints, external shocks, and broader economic conditions. One of the economic conditions we focus on in this book is interregional inequality. Although conceptually (discussed in Chap. 2) it has been shown that the effectiveness of monetary policy and interregional inequality have a symbiotic/interdependent relationship, what did the evidence show?

In terms of the number of business units and labor absorption, the trade sector has been dominant in many regions throughout Indonesia. Given the existing high degree of interregional inequality, most credit borrowers operate in retail trade, and many of them rely on bank credit for financing. The retail trade is also where most local labor works. As detailed in Chap. 3, the productivity of this sector is low and declining.

In many less developed regions, especially those outside of Jawa and eastern Indonesia, manufacturing is only a small part of the economy. These regions typically cannot produce most of the goods that local consumers need (especially durable goods and other basic goods). Many of the goods that retailers sell are not produced locally; they are purchased outside the region. Depending on the type and quality, many of them were purchased from Jawa. This is the reason why data on the high loan-to-deposit ratio outside Jawa could give a false impression that regions have ample liquidity to finance their development needs, i.e., the higher the loan-to-deposit ratio, the greater the region's capacity to grow. Obviously, this is a faulty deduction. Most of the credit from local banks was not spent locally. Some banks indicated that around 80–100% of credits they allocated were spent elsewhere, mostly in Jawa, intensifying the spatial concentration of money supply.

In any case, there is a clear relationship between the credit of the local bank and inequality. The real critical factor here is the existing (initial) high degree of interregional inequality, where many less developed regions are unable to produce goods that local consumers need. Only developed regions have the capacity to produce those goods. This is a typical feature of an economy with a high degree of spatial inequality. Consequently, data on total national credit obscure the spatial distribution of money supply, and the resulting aggregate national output does not account for the worsening interregional distribution. The reality is that the allocation of credit driven by monetary policy has reinforced the high inequality that was initial between regions.

Since the pass-through of monetary policy is dependent on the degree of spatial inequality, the higher the inequality, the more likely the policy channels work less uniformly across regions, and the less synchronized the response to the policy will be. As a result, the outcome of aggregate variables targeted by monetary policy (GDP growth, inflation, unemployment) cannot be consistently realized, reducing the effectiveness of the policy. We have previously observed evidence of some ineffectiveness of BI policy, and in Chap. 3 we have shown that interregional inequality in Indonesia is high and is still rising. The discussions in the next Section argue that the simultaneous occurrence of these two observations is real, and the evidence of causality is exposed in the Section that follows.

5.2 Test of Independence

We begin with an exploratory attempt to see if there is a relationship between the objectives of the BI policy and the interregional inequality. To examine the three target variables, we use heat maps to detect the continuous gradation of the relationship. Denoting the level of the Williamson index (WI) by the intensity of the color in the heatmaps, and using the moving average (MA) of the debt/GDP ratio as a control variable, Fig. 5.4 Panel A shows the heatmap using WI based on regional GDP/capita and Panel B using WI based on regional consumption per capita.

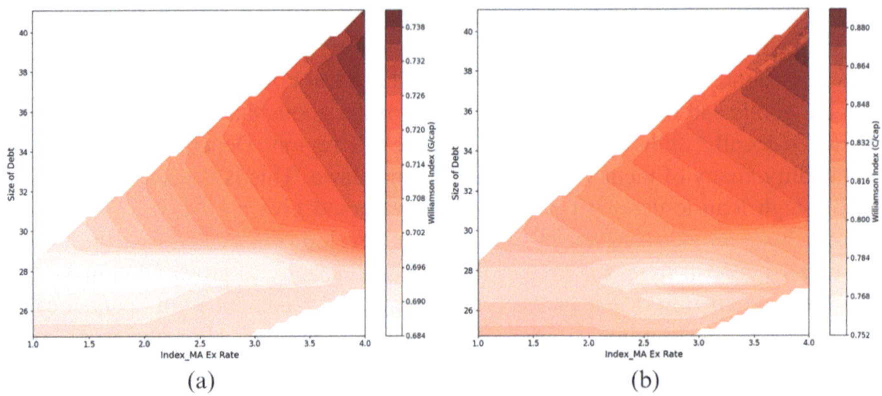

Fig. 5.4 Heatmap of Williamson Index (WI) based on regional per-capita GDP, per-capita consumption, and the exchange rate, using debt size and exchange rate as control variables. (**a**) WI based on Regional GRDP/cap. (**b**) WI based on Regional Consumption/cap. *Source*: Author's drawing

The only association we could detect rather clearly from those figures was between WI and exchange rate. The high depreciation of the exchange rate occurred at a high level of WI and also at a high level of debt/GDP. Alternatively stated, at any level of debt/GDP, the higher the interregional inequality the weaker the rupiah would be, as shown by the darker color (rightward of the graph). However, note that when the debt/GDP level was high, there were cases where low inequality coincided with high inflation.

If we used the gap instead of the level of the three target variables, there are more cases that show closer relationships. Figure 5.5 provides a visualization of the association between interregional inequality and variables of interest. It is clearly shown that a weaker exchange rate (rightward of the x-axis) coincided with a higher interregional inequality (darker color), regardless of the control variables being used. More specifically, a larger fiscal deficit, a wider current account deficit, and larger debt occurred at the same time with a greater depreciation of the Rupiah and a more unequal distribution between regions. The figure also shows a fairly close association between higher inequality and lower GDP growth regardless of the choice of control variables. Since we did not find a relationship between inflation and inequality, the heatmaps for inflation are not shown here.

Similar results are obtained when we use consumption per capita as the basis for the WI measure (lower part of Fig. 5.5). Hence, based on heatmaps, there is an early indication that interregional inequality may have some bearing on the effectiveness of monetary policy.

Although heatmaps show visual clarity of the association between variables, they cannot provide a formal statistical measure (statistical significance) of the relationship. For that purpose and to help determine whether the relationships are due to just a chance or not, the Chi-square is used. The null hypothesis (H_0) is that

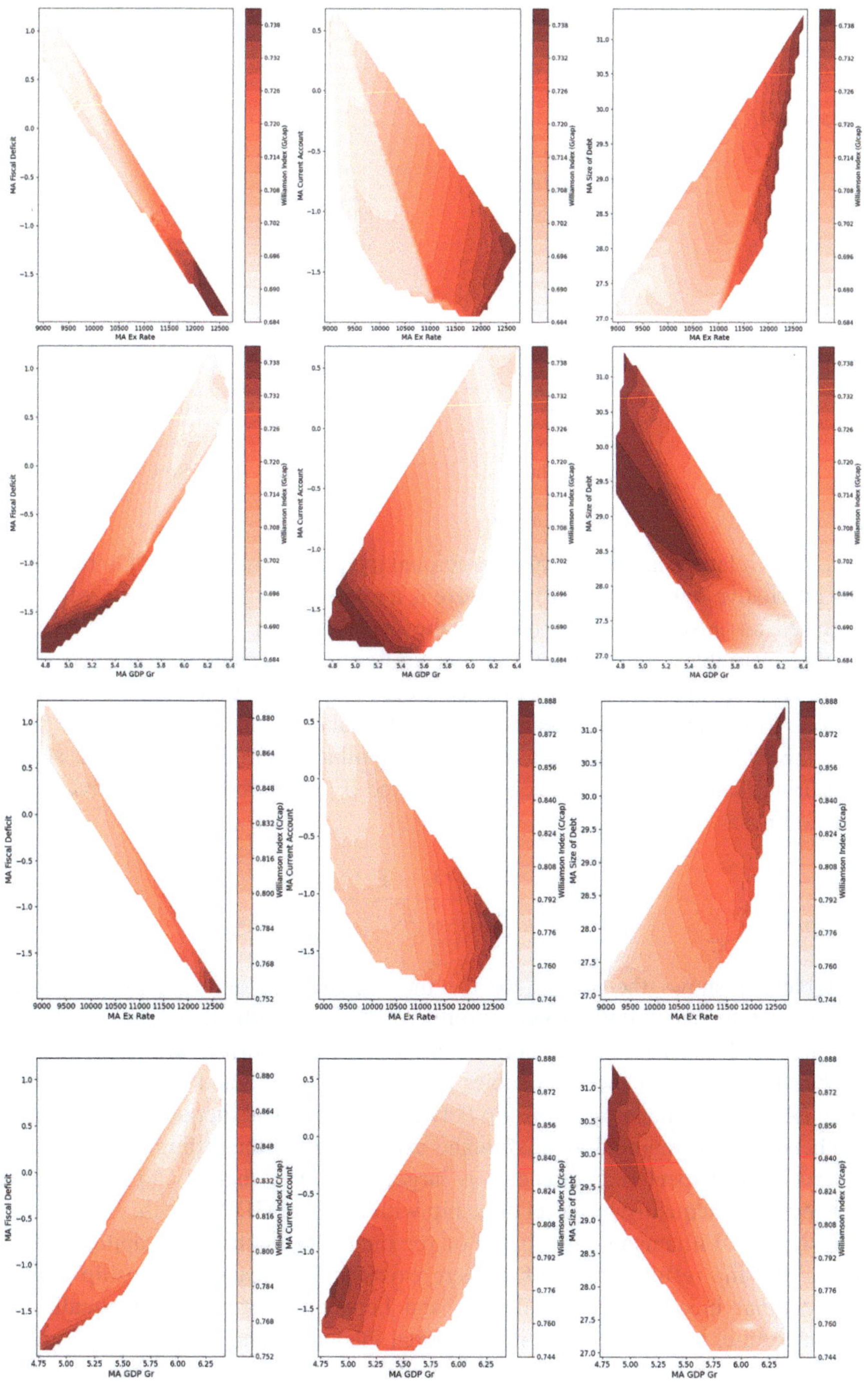

Fig. 5.5 Heatmap of Williamson Index (WI) based on regional per-capita GDP, per-capita consumption, and the gaps of exchange rate and GDP growth, using fiscal deficit, debt size and exchange rate as control variables. (**a**) WI based on regional GDP/cap. (**b**) WI based on regional Consumption/cap. *Source*: Author's drawing

Table 5.1 Inflation, GDP growth, and exchange rate versus Williamson index for GDP/cap: test of independence. *Source*: Author's calculations

		WI GDP/cap	
Inflation MA gap		Low WI	Large WI
	Low	11	24
	Large	17	4
	Fischer test	0.0007	Significant
GDP growth MA gap		Low WI	Large WI
	Low	15	14
	Large	13	14
	Fischer Test	1	Not significant
Exhange rate MA gap		Low WI	Large WI
	Low	22	6
	Large	6	28
	Fischer test	0.0000000004	Significant

there is no relationship between interregional inequality and the variable of interest. The alternative hypothesis (H_a) is: There is a relationship between the two.

Based on information and data on the gaps between the actual and target of the three variables, we grouped them according to the category 'low' and 'high', where 'low' ('high') refers to the cases where the value of the respective variable is lower (higher) than the mean average. We subsequently compared the results with the Williamson index (classified in a similar way). The chi-square statistic measuring the difference between the expected (E_i) and observed (O_i) frequencies is as follows:

$$\sum_i \frac{(O_i - E_i)^2}{E_i}$$

Table 5.1 shows the results for the moving average of the gaps in inflation, exchange rate, and GDP growth, compared to the Williamson index based on regional GDP per capita. The corresponding results of Fisher-test is displayed at the bottom. Based on the frequencies shown in the Table and the Fisher statistic, there exists a significant relationship between interregional inequality and inflation, and between interregional inequality and exchange rate (the difference between the observed and expected frequencies is large). However, there is no evidence that interregional inequality has a relationship with regional GDP growth.

Using the Williamson index based on regional consumption per capita, Table 5.2 shows that the results are similar: there exists a significant relationship between interregional inequality and inflation, and between interregional inequality and exchange rate, but not between interregional inequality and regional GDP growth. Hence, based on the results of the Chi-square tests, there is an indication that the target variables of the BI (inflation and exchange rate) have a relationship with the degree of inequality between the regions of Indonesia.

Table 5.2 Inflation, GDP growth, and exchange rate versus Williamson index for consumption/cap: test of independence. *Source*: Author's calculations

		WI C/cap	
Inflation MA gap		Low WI	Large WI
	Low	15	20
	Large	17	4
	Fischer test	0.006	Significant
GDP growth MA gap		Low WI	Large WI
	Low	19	10
	Large	13	14
	Fischer test	0.28	Not significant
Exhange rate MA gap		Low WI	Large WI
	Low	22	10
	Large	10	24
	Fischer test	0.00000003	Significant

It is interesting to note that the results of the heatmaps and the Chi-square are the same for the exchange rate but different for the other two variables. More specifically, there exists a close relationship between inequality and GDP growth according to heat maps but not the Chi-square, and a close relationship between inequality and inflation according to the Chi-square but not heat maps.

5.3 Mixed-Effect Model

Although Chi-square tests are useful for assessing associations in categorical data and heatmaps show the visualization of relationships, they do not account for other influencing variables. To the extent that causality always involves complex interactions among several confounding variables, and the strength of direction and the significance of relationships matter, a specific regression technique is subsequently used to test the nature and intensity of interregional inequality in influencing the effectiveness of monetary policy.[1]

Since money supply can be both an instrument and an effect of monetary policy, we first need to determine the regional variable directly affected by money supply. The level of credit is what we choose for the following reasons. Regional credit serves as a useful indicator of regional effects on national money supply because it reflects borrowing and lending activities within a region, which in turn influences the local money supply: higher credit growth indicates higher contribution to

[1] Regression technique also offers diagnostic tools to evaluate model performance to ensure robust causality analysis that heatmaps and Chi-square cannot do. The latter lack mechanisms to assess the quality of the revealed association.

the national money supply.[2] The relationship between the two, however, varies between regions due to differences in economic structures, financial systems, and institutional setting. If the growth of regional credit aligns with the national monetary policy goals (e.g. price stability and growth), there is a strong connection between regional credit and national money supply; vice versa if credit growth does not align with the policy goals. Most importantly, regional credit can be used as one of the most important indicators to examine how effectively monetary policy is transmitted between different regions. In selecting the econometric technique to use, therefore, we need to account for differences across regions.

First, we run a standard money supply equation (M2) where the output and interest rates are the important explanatory variables at the national level, from which we obtain the estimated money supply (p_M2). This is Part-1 of the model. We then run the regional credit regression, in which the estimated money supply is used as one of the independent variables (Part 2).[3] To capture the effect of interregional inequality, we then run a similar model but added two interactive terms for money supply: first, the interactive term with COVID dummy to gauge the effect of money supply on regional credit during the pandemic and second, the interactive term with the Williamson index to capture the effect of interregional inequality. Since we use two types of Williamson Index, one is based on regional per capita GDP (labeled WG) and another on regional per capita consumption (WC), there are two equations with interactive terms: one using WG (Part-3A) and another using WC (Part-3B). The full model is the following.

Part-1:

$$\text{M2}_t = \beta_0 + \beta_1 \text{Y\_Nation}_t + \beta_2 \text{M2}_{t-1} + \epsilon_t$$

Part-2:

$$\text{Credit}_{it} = \beta_0 + \beta_1 \text{p\_M2}_t + \beta_2 \text{COVID}_t + \beta_3 Y_{it} + \beta_4 \text{Credit}_{i(t-1)} + u_{it} + \epsilon_t$$

Part-3A:

$$\text{Credit}_{it} = \beta_0 + \beta_1 \text{p\_M2}_t + \beta_2 \text{COVID}_t + \beta_3 Y_{it} + \beta_4 \text{Credit}_{i(t-1)} + \gamma_1 (\text{p\_M2}_t \times \text{COVID}_t) + \gamma_2 (\text{p\_M2}_t \times WG) + u_{it} + \epsilon_t$$

Part-3B:

$$\text{Credit}_{it} = \beta_0 + \beta_1 \text{p\_M2}_t + \beta_2 \text{COVID}_t + \beta_3 Y_{it} + \beta_4 \text{Credit}_{i(t-1)} + \gamma_1 (\text{p\_M2}_t \times \text{COVID}_t) + \gamma_2 (\text{p\_M2}_t \times WC) + u_{it} + \epsilon_t$$

Random Effect:

$$u_{it} = \delta_0 + \delta_1 \text{p\_M2}_{it} + \delta_2 \text{COVID}_{it} + \delta_3 Y_{it} + \delta_4 \text{Credit}_{i(t-1)}$$

where M2_t is the money supply (p_M2 is the predicted money supply based on Part-1), Y_Nation_t is the national output, Y_t is the regional output, Credit_t is regional credit, COVID_t is a dummy variable, WG is the Williamson index based on regional GDP per capita, WC is the Williamson index based on regional per capita consumption, u_{it} is the random effect component for province i at time t capturing

[2] Note that some factors other than regional credit may also play role in determining the regional effect on the national money supply; e.g., migration, inter-regional trade, fiscal policies.

[3] Since the quarterly data being used covered the 2010q1-2023q4 period, we included a dummy variable for COVID pandemic in the equation (the expected sign of the coefficient is negative).

unobserved heterogeneity, and ϵ_t is the idiosyncratic error term accounting for unexplained residual variation.

Since evaluating the role of interregional inequality is our primary interest, attention is directed towards the second interactive term (γ_2). Obviously, the coefficients of M2 in the model with interaction and without interaction are different. The one without the interaction reflects an unconditional effect of M2 on regional credit, and the one with the interaction reflects a conditional effect. The difference is explained by the interaction term. The idea of such a specification is to find out whether the presence of WG and WC had a significant influence on the effect of money supply on regional credit. Using the coefficient of the second interactive term, we adopt the following strategy.

If that coefficient (γ_2) is zero, the interaction term disappears, that is, the effect of M2 on regional credit is just equal to the coefficient of M2 in the regression. This is a standard result of the money supply equation when no interregional inequality is considered (ignoring spatial inequality). It is when the value of γ_2 is non-zero that our hypothesis becomes relevant. It highlights a critical nuance where the effects of M2 are not uniform across regions.

If γ_2 is positive, we simply enhance the coefficient of M2 by this positive coefficient, which implies that the effect of monetary policy (reflected in M2) on regional credit increases as the interregional inequality worsens. Alternatively, given the money supply, when the interregional inequality increases, the regional credit also increases. In an environment of high inequality, this could happen when few developed regions show heightened credit activities, driving the overall lending trend.

When the coefficient γ_2 becomes negative, it suggests that the worsening of the interregional inequality will reduce the effectiveness of the policy. This is the key hypothesis that we postulate. As inequality increases, the positive effect of M2 on regional credit weakens. When inequality continues to rise and reaches a high level, the interaction term could become large enough in magnitude to offset the positive impact of M2 without the interactive term (positive coefficient β_1), potentially making the total effect of M2 on regional credit initially diminish, then reaches zero, and eventually turns negative. This could happen because when interregional inequality is high, financial access is often concentrated in only a few developed regions, so that when central bank raises money supply, the increased supply does not flow into broad credit expansion (across regions), reducing the effectiveness of the policy. On the other hand, when the interregional inequality is low, monetary policy is more effective as the increase in the money supply has a positive impact on regional credit.

Therefore, if our hypothesis holds (γ is negative), an important policy implication would be for monetary authority to incorporate spatial indicators when formulating monetary policy in order to increase the effectiveness of the policy. Although reducing the interregional inequality itself is obviously preferable, such a policy is outside the mandate of monetary authority. However, it is one of the most important policies to take, especially if instability is to be avoided and greater national growth is to be achieved. Hence, policy makers and social planners need to

Table 5.3 Results of the M2 regression

	M2
Y_Nation	0.3121***
	(0.0220)
i	−19.9768***
	(3.6511)
M2 (−1)	−0.8179***
	(0.0132)
Constant	68.60131**
	(31.3345)
Number of observations	1870
Adj R-squared	0.9930

Notes: **, and *** denote statistical significance at the 10%, 5%, and 1% levels, respectively. Standard errors are shown in parentheses

pay more serious attention to efforts to reduce inequality between regions. As argued in the preceding chapter, to be effective, such efforts should consider the local need and the prevailing institutions, especially when they involve making regulations and allocating funds for regional investment and infrastructure.

Let us now look at the results of the model using Indonesian data. We applied a mixed-effects model in which the fixed-effects part is represented by the money supply, and the random-effects part captures the variability in bank credit across regions. To ensure better reliability of the variance estimates, we adopted the restricted maximum likelihood (REML) method, which is best applied for cases with small datasets or a limited number of regions, such as in our case. This method does not affect the consistency of fixed effect estimates or the coefficient of money supply, but it provides better estimates for random effects and their variances (the focus of REML is precisely on how variance components are estimated).[4]

The results of applying the above approach are shown in Tables 5.3, 5.4, and 5.5. The fixed effect part (money supply equation) is quite straightforward, where all coefficients are significant and show the expected signs (numbers inside the brackets are the standard error). In Table 5.5, the random effect parameters show that the variability of the effect of regional output and M2 without interactions across regions is small, suggesting that the random variability associated with this predictor is negligible in all three models. That is, the variability of the effect is stable and highly consistent between regions. The values for COVID are around 2.6, indicating that COVID introduces relatively high variability between observations. However, although the intercept with and without interactive terms is very small, it varies significantly, where the highest is in the case without interactive terms, suggesting

[4] Unlike in maximum likelihood (ML), the variance estimate for the random effect (regional variability) in REML is lower, reflecting REML's adjustment for bias. On the other hand, the standard error for the fixed effects (e.g. money supply) is larger because the REML estimates are more conservative, ensuring a better reliability of the variance estimates.

Table 5.4 Results of mixed-effect models with and without interactive terms

Fixed-effects parameters	(1)	(2)	(3)
p_M2	0.0081**	0.0083***	0.0003*
	(0.0035)	(0.0028)	(0.0002)
COVID	−19.3721***	−9.8029***	−1.8024**
	(4.3279)	(3.3705)	(0.7183)
Y	0.1475***	0.1510***	0.1540***
	(0.0234)	(0.0235)	(0.0234)
Credit (−1)	0.8862***	0.8827***	0.8784***
	(0.0167)	(0.0166)	(0.0163)
Constant	−3.8058**	−2.9807***	−1.3721**
	(1.6300)	(1.0869)	(0.6370)
Interaction term			
p_M2 × COVID	0.0026***	0.0012***	
	(0.0006)	(0.0004)	
p_M2 × WC	−0.0089**		
	(0.0039)		
p_M2 × WG		−0.0108***	
		(0.0036)	

*$0.05 \le p < 0.1$, **$0.01 \le p < 0.05$, ***$p < 0.01$

Table 5.5 Results of random effects parameters

Random-effects parameters		Estimate	
sd(p_M2)	8.14e-12	1.01e-10	2.06e-13
	(0.0000)	(0.0000)	(0.0000)
sd(Y)	0.0698	0.0698	0.0710
	(0.0000)	(0.0000)	(0.0000)
sd(COVID)	2.6289	2.6456	2.6286
	(0.0000)	(0.0000)	(0.0000)
sd(Credit (-1))	0.0327	0.0323	0.0327
	(0.0000)	(0.0000)	(0.0000)
sd(Constant)	5.17e-07	7.17e-06	3.45e-08
	(0.0000)	(0.0000)	(0.0000)
sd(Residual)	6.3349	6.3282	6.3606
	(0.0000)	(0.0000)	(0.0000)
Number of obs/groups	55	55	55
Number of groups	34	34	34
LR test vs. linear model			
$\chi^2(5)$	256.31	259.62	283.05
Prob > $\chi^2(5)$	0.0000	0.0000	0.0000

that the variation in baseline credit across regions becomes less pronounced if we include the interactive term. Finally, the residual variation appears to be quite large, meaning that the unexplained variation in the data remains at a relatively high level. This is expected because our main purpose here is to focus on whether or not interregional inequality significantly influences the effectiveness of monetary policy, rather than finding the best model for regional credit. For the latter, other relevant factors should certainly be included. Overall, the results of random effects suggest that COVID and residual error contribute significantly to variability, but other predictors exhibit low random-effect variability, implying that they function more as fixed effects, with limited random fluctuations between regions.

When comparing the case of with and without interactive terms, the intercepts in both cases are negative, with a larger negative value for the case with interactive terms (Table 5.4). This suggests that in some regions there might be a general structural weakness in credit availability. Note that here we refer to the mixed-effect results using WG (the signs of the coefficients from regression using WC are basically similar). When interactions are included, the coefficient for money supply is also higher compared to the case without interactions (0.008 versus 0.0003), suggesting that once we include interregional inequality in the model, the exclusive effect of money supply on regional credit given the interactive term is strengthened. However, it is one thing to consider inequality to evaluate the effect of M2, but it is an entirely different matter to account for the specific extent or degree of inequality. This issue becomes clearer when the coefficient of the interactive terms involving M2 and inequality is negative (see below).

The negative coefficient for COVID indicates that the pandemic had led to credit contraction. The devastating impacts of the pandemic across all regions intensified the contraction when the interactive term was included as the negative coefficient increased.

Next are the effect of the interactive terms. The coefficient (γ is positive for the M2 and COVID interaction, implying that given COVID, the effect of the money supply on regional credit is amplified. Monetary policy had a stronger effect in boosting regional credit during the pandemic, where liquidity injections, stimulus measures, or expansionary monetary policies were particularly effective in mitigating the credit contraction caused by the COVID shock.

The next interactive term is the most important one for our hypothesis. Here, we distinguish the result from the use of WG and WC. The coefficient γ is negative (-0.0108 and -0.0089 for using WG and WC, respectively), implying that as the interregional inequality increased, the positive effect of the money supply on regional credit weakened. Recalling what has been described above, this indicates that the effectiveness of monetary policy was dampened by the large development gap between regions.[5] Indeed, in a high inequality environment like Indonesia,

[5] There have been numerous quantitative studies to evaluate the effectiveness of monetary policy, e.g., Primus (2016). But only in more recent years has the effect of interaction between monetary policy and inequality received greater attention. McKay and Wolf (2023) looked at the link between

financial access is often concentrated in certain regions (mainly in Jawa), so that when the BI raised the money supply, the increased supply did not flow into broad credit expansion. In other words, had the development gap between the regions been small (low WG or WC), the BI's monetary policy had been more effective, as the money supply would generate a positive impact on regional credit.

From a longer-term perspective, if this issue is not addressed, there is a possibility that spiraling effects will occur. As already elaborated in earlier chapters, given Indonesia's high interregional inequality, the current allocation of credit to less developed regions has not been fully beneficial to local development, as most of the credit was spent elsewhere outside of the regions. In this context, if local credits are dependent on the prevailing monetary policy, the results discussed above indicate that the policy tends to aggravate rather than mitigate the inequality between regions. The widening interregional inequality discussed in Chap. 3 can be reinforced by this development, leaving less developed regions outside of Jawa and especially Eastern Indonesia with lower-than-desirable liquidity. This is despite the fact that, compared to Jawa, they are much more in need of financing local economic activities. As a result, interregional inequality persists, as does the ineffectiveness of monetary policy.

The diminished effectiveness of monetary policy caused by inequality sets in motion a feedback loop: Ineffectiveness amplifies inequality, and inequality causes policy ineffectiveness, perpetuating a vicious cycle. Over time, this escalating cycle can snowball, worsening disparities and compounding the challenges far beyond the current ones. Attempts to reach monetary targets and maximize growth with stability are hindered by a "Broken Ladder" of interregional inequality.

References

De Groot, O., Hauptmeier, S., Holm-Hadulla, F., & Nikalexi, K. (2023). Monetary policy and regional inequality. *ECB Working Paper Series*, No. 2385, December.

Dossche, M., Slačálek, J., & Wolswijk, G. (2021). Monetary policy and inequality. *ECB Economic Bulletin* (2).

Francis, N., Owyang, M. T., & Sekhposyan, T. (2011). The local effects of monetary policy. *Federal Reserve Bank of St. Louis Working Paper*, 2009-048. https://doi.org/10.20955/wp.2009.048.

McKay, A., & Wolf, C. K. (2023). Monetary policy and inequality. *Journal of Economic Perspectives, 37*(1), 121–144.

Primus, K. (2016). The effectiveness of monetary policy in small open economies: An empirical investigation. *IMF Working Paper*, WP/16/189.

---

monetary policy and inequality, and Dossche et al. (2021) studied the link between monetary policy and regional inequality. The impact of monetary policy on regional inequality was studied by Francis et al. (2011) at the St Louis Federal Reserves, and by De Groot et al. (2023) at the ECB.

Chapter 6
Go Behind the Wall

We have discussed in Chap. 2 that the sources of heterogeneous effects of monetary policy across regions can be viewed from two different perspectives: different structures and characteristics across regions and different behavior of local banks towards credit allocation. In both perspectives, the magnitude and directions of the heterogeneous effects depend on the period under analysis, and the accuracy of the estimates of the effect crucially depends on the adopted measure (Romer & Romer, 2004). In fact, as revealed in the preceding chapter, the responses of the regions to monetary policy, observed through regional credit allocation, are quite different from the average response. The responses in one region are not the same as those in other regions.

The nature of monetary policy also matters. Many studies have shown that monetary tightening leads to a persistent decrease in regional output and income, in which less developed regions tend to feel the contractionary effect more than developed regions (see Carlino & DeFina, 1998; Pizzuto, 2020). Monetary loosening leads to an increase in regional production and income, but the regional distribution of benefits is uncertain, depending on the industry mix of the region, the size of banks, and the share of small and medium enterprises (SMEs) in the region. Regions with a large share of interest rates-sensitive sectors, such as construction and manufacturing, tend to benefit more, and those with many smaller banks could also gain a relatively greater benefit from the policy because smaller banks are more limited in their ability to find alternatives to nondeposit sources of funding (bank lending channel; see Kashyap & Jeremy, 1994).

In regions where most business activities are of the SMEs type, a loosening policy may not have significant impacts. Although theoretically small businesses rely more on bank loans, the reality on the ground shows that in many developing countries, most small businesses face greater obstacles compared to big companies in getting loans. Their access to bank credit is far more limited. For example, the share of credits for SME over GDP in Indonesia is around 6–7%, among the smallest in the world (see Azis, 2024). However, SMEs make up around 99% of the country's

I. J. Azis, *Monetary Whispers Across Space*,
https://doi.org/10.1007/978-981-95-4625-1_6

business establishment. The impact of monetary policy in this case is minimal. Typically, small businesses face higher information and transaction costs to meet their credit needs (Bernanke & Gertler, 1995).

But what distinguishes the structural approach from the behavioral approach in analyzing the heterogeneous effects of monetary policy across regions is the time frame and context. The structural approach focuses on long-term systemic factors that influence the effect of monetary policy on regional disparities. It takes a more macrolevel view of regional disparities, where structural elements such as regional economic structure, industry composition, and banking concentration must be examined. The behavioral approach, on the other hand, offers a more microlevel, more granular real-time analysis of how regions respond differently to monetary policy, by emphasizing short-term behaviors of banks, such as their lending practices, deposit mobilization strategies, and responses to market conditions, and of consumers (their spending patterns), and of the business sector (their investment decisions).

Hence, the structural approach examines indicators such as loan-to-deposit ratio (LDR) from a macroeconomic or systemic perspective, by focusing on the long-term trends and structural factors that influence the ratio, such as regulatory frameworks, economic conditions, and the overall stability of the banking system. In contrast, the behavioral approach recognizes that banks can adjust their LDR based on factors such as customer behavior, competition, and liquidity needs. The money supply is endogenously influenced by the behavior of the bank. To evaluate the effect of monetary policy under the behavioral approach, therefore, we need to examine factors that affect this behavior. And since lending transactions involve lenders and borrowers, this also means including factors that affect the behavior of borrowers. One of such factors is the "liquidity preference". The question is: What is the indicator that best reflects liquidity preference and what are the factors that could affect such preference?

6.1 Data on Liquidity Preference

Conceptually, liquidity preference can be detected, at least in part, by comparing bank lending and bank deposits. If the credit-to-deposit ratio of the local banks is low, the possibility is either banks have limited reserves, unhealthy balance sheet (e.g., high nonperforming loans and low capital adequacy), high operating expenses, or they are simply being risk averse. Under such circumstances, a cursory interpretation would be: banks have a high liquidity preference, as they need to have enough liquid assets to meet short-term obligations.

But credit transactions are the result of a two-party agreement: the lenders and the borrowers. The low credit deposit ratio could also be caused by the high liquidity preference of potential borrowers due to a number of factors, e.g., a lack of business opportunities or low market confidence. In the case of SMEs, cultural factors could also play an important role, e.g., credit borrowing is seen as a sign of moral weakness or financial irresponsibility (social stigma), prefer to borrow from family, friends, or community members (social capital), or unwilling to accept interest-based transaction (religious belief). Basically, some members of the society may not be willing to incur debt by borrowing from banks. Other cases of limited borrowing we found during the field survey were driven by bad past experience dealing with banks or being blacklisted by banks (trust factor). All of these will result in weak demand for bank credit, making the loan-to-deposit ratio (LDR) low. However, since such cases reflect more of the demand side, a low ratio can be seen as a sign of the high liquidity preference of borrowers.

In reality, the observed credit deposit ratio is an outcome of the interdependence between the supply and demand for credit. It is difficult to disentangle factors that reflect supply and demand, let alone separate them. One thing is certain, if both banks and the public have a strong liquidity preference, the loan-to-deposit ratio would be very low, as they prefer to hold cash or any liquid assets.

How is this issue related to the alternative approach to analyze the different loan-to-deposit ratio between Jawa and non-Jawa? If a low credit deposit ratio is driven by banks being constrained by their reserves, this can be more in line with the assumption of structural approach where money supply is determined nationally (exogenously) and the distribution across regions depends on the economic structure of the regions. As explained in Chap. 2, this is very different from the 'behavioral approach' where it is the behavior of local banks that determines the allocation of local credit (depending on local needs). The national money supply will adjust accordingly (endogenous money). In the end, under the two approaches, not only the impact of monetary policy on the economy may not be the same, but the impact on regional development and interregional inequality may also be different.

If local banks are not restricted by reserves and their decisions are based on real potential or regional needs, regional and national growth would have been greater. If, at the same time, regulatory instruments are strictly imposed to ensure that local banks including those in less developed regions meet the credit needs of local communities, for example, through credit guarantee, tax or capital incentives, tiered regulation, or reduced compliance costs, the growth and welfare gap between developed and less developed regions would have been narrowed too.

What do the data say? Nationally, as far as bank financing is concerned, Indonesia has always had a surplus of savings where total credit is greater than total bank savings, that is, the loan-to-deposit ratio is less-than 100%; see Fig. 6.1.[1] Breaking down into Jawa and Non-Jawa, however, the differences in those two regions are apparent. In Jawa, most banks have recorded savings greater than credit, while outside of Jawa, the opposite holds (Fig. 6.2).[2] From the results of our field survey

[1] Since banks deposit is the largest component of saving, the widely used term is loan-to-deposit ratio. With few exceptions, in most regions, the largest share of credit was allocated to working capital, followed by consumption. Credit for investment usually has the lowest share.

[2] In both Jawa and non-Jawa the largest portion of bank credit is for working capital, but the regional distribution indicates that in outside Jawa the largest share of credit is for consumption (40.3%). Similarly, by breaking Indonesia down into West and East, the largest credit in the West is for working capital (46. 1%), while in the East it is for consumption (47.5%). Interestingly, the average interest rates for consumption credit in Non-Java (11.89%) are lower than in Java (12.55%), and those for investment and working capital are higher in Non-Java.

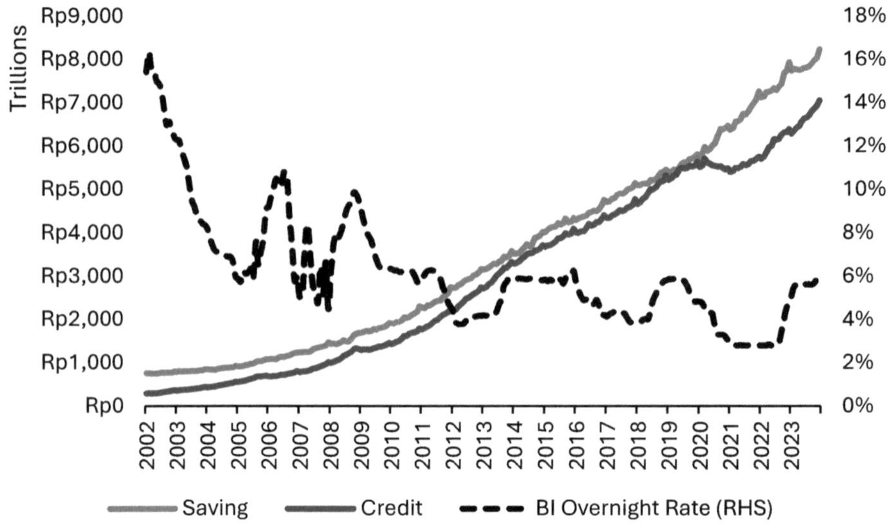

Fig. 6.1 Loan-to-deposit ratio: total Indonesia. *Source*: Author's construction based on data from SEKI Bank Indonesia

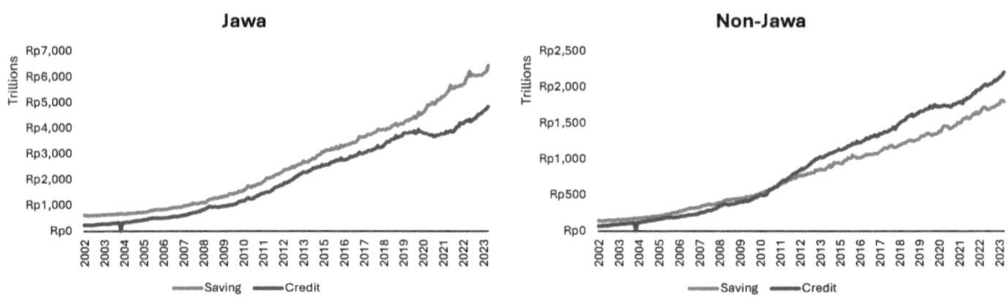

Fig. 6.2 Loan-to-deposit ratio: Jawa and Non-Jawa. *Source*: Author's calculation based on data from SEKDA Bank Indonesia

(discussed later), this is consistent with what the respondents have expressed. Unlike bankers outside Jawa, those in Jawa ranked the preference for liquidity as the highest. For banks outside Jawa, the results varied. Some consider profitability more important than liquidity; others consider liquidity more important than profitability.

Classified into four groups, state-owned banks, people's credit bank (*Bank Perekonomian Rakyat*, BPR), regional development bank (*Bank Pembangunan Daerah*, BPD) and private banks, the first three categories of banks outside of Jawa place profitability as the main priority, while the latter category considers liquidity the most important key performance indicator (KPI). Similarly to what was found in other countries, the level of development or the size of the bank also influence the ranking of KPI (see Duran & Erdem, 2014).

In trying to delineate the factors behind the above regional distribution and the liquidity preference of banks, it is important to link the issue with the specific characteristics of Indonesia's financial system, especially the banking sector. In general, Indonesia's financial sector is typical of many lower middle-income countries. It has grown steadily and made improvements in some areas, especially after the 1997 Asian Financial Crisis. It is heavily bank-dependent, has limited inclusion and is highly concentrated, where almost half of the total assets of banks belong to the top five banks, and three quarters of the capital market capitalization are owned by less than 10% of all listed companies. Although the country's banking sector has a high capital adequacy ratio (CAR), more than 20%, where around 90% of the available capital is a category of tier 1, it is highly segmented. Combined with a small and shallow capital market, this segmented banking sector makes the cost of intermediation high, and the interbank and money markets cannot really function optimally. The regulatory structure and framework are fragmented, albeit gradually improving. The excessive reliance of banks on short-term sources of funding and the illiquidity of capital markets lead to high interest rates, net interest margin (NIM), and bond yields. Among major ASEAN countries, Indonesia has the highest of those three indicators (Azis, 2018).

Given the above features, it is less likely that the low loan-to-deposit ratio of most banks in Jawa was due to limited reserves and low CAR. They may have high operating expenses, and some may simply be too risk-averse. To some extent, the insurance provided by Lembaga Penjamin Simpanan, LPS (Indonesian Deposit Insurance Company, IDIC), should also remove the fear of liquidity problems.

On the demand side, most of the regions in Jawa are more developed than those outside Jawa. Social capital and cultural factors are not as significant as in most regions outside of Jawa. Many big companies did not rely on bank credit (self-funded). Even if they did get credit from banks, the amount was likely less than the actual spending. That may contribute to the limited size of total bank credit. Indeed, Indonesia's bank credit to the private sector is just slightly above 30% of GDP, much lower than in many other emerging markets (roughly 50%). Based solely on this fact, the country's financial system is less developed compared to some of its peers.

Another potential factor is the preference of banks to hold government bonds as safe assets. More-than 30% of total government bond is held by banks, and the amount has been steadily increasing especially after the COVID 19 pandemic, during which the government raised the bond issuance multiple times to finance various COVID-related expenditures. This also explains why the CAR of banks in Indonesia is relatively high.

There are a number of possible explanations for why the loan-to-deposit ratio of banks outside of Jawa is high. From the bank's perspective, since the only available source of funding is the deposit of customers (owing to limited access to the capital markets), they must focus on getting more clients to deposit their money there. It may also be the case that the enforcement of regulatory environment outside Jawa is less stringent, allowing banks to maintain higher LDRs without facing significant liquidity risks. For local government-owned banks (BPDs), the pressure should be less since they can secure a captive market of government employees. But even some of the aggressive non-BPD managed to get some government employees to keep deposits in their banks and lend out a larger share of their deposits.

6.2 Bank's Perceptions

Despite all the potential explanations for the high or low loan-to-deposit ratio described above, it is impossible to conclude with high certainty that the low (high) ratio really indicates a high (low) liquidity preference. Revealing the true preference or behavior of the bank is not an easy task, as it can vary widely from bank to bank, and it can be influenced by various factors other than the technical reasons mentioned above. Factors such as the working environment, individual experiences, and social interactions with borrowers also matter. Not to mention the distinctive characteristics and genetics-driven behavior of individuals in charge that make each of them unique and different, including in responding to a situation like a change in monetary policy.

This is the reason why we decided to conduct a survey and interact directly with local bankers and other stakeholders to find the relative importance of liquidity preference from their perspective and what they perceive about the day-to-day operations in terms of such a preference. With the right questions to ask and the use of a proper method to capture banks' perceptions, we should be better able to reveal what they perceive about their liquidity preference. Direct participation during the field survey helps us understand the subjects better (this author strongly believes that when we don't know what is behind the wall, "Go Behind The Wall"). After combining the results with the data on the loan-to-deposit ratio, we could gauge the overall level of bank liquidity preference. The bulk of discussions in this Section is devoted to the framework, questionnaires, and the results of the survey.

6.2.1 Survey Framework

Realizing the important role of individual characteristics in expressing their perceptions and cognizant of the fact that humans are always biased because all perceptions and cognitions are grounded in personal history (human bias serves as a fundamental protective mechanism for humans), we conducted the survey using a specific approach that allows some biases but maintains some degrees of consistency. The types of questions we raised are put in a pairwise-comparisons way as in the Analytic Hierarchy Process (AHP) approach. In such an approach, we allow intangible factors to be part of the criteria together with tangible factors (bank and financial indicators) to determine the priority ranking of the bank's liquidity preference.

We grouped the relevant elements into three parts (clusters). Priorities, key performance indicator (KPI) and policies. Six elements were listed in Priorities: regular saving (K1), syariah-based saving (K2), regular credit (K3), syariah-based credit (K4), regular placement (K5) and syariah-based placement (K6). In KPI, we list three elements: liquidity (S1), solvability (S2), and profitability (S3), and in the Policies group, the listed elements were capital strengthening (P1), improvements in governance/human resource (P2), adoption of digital technology (P3), and relaxation of bank regulations (P4).

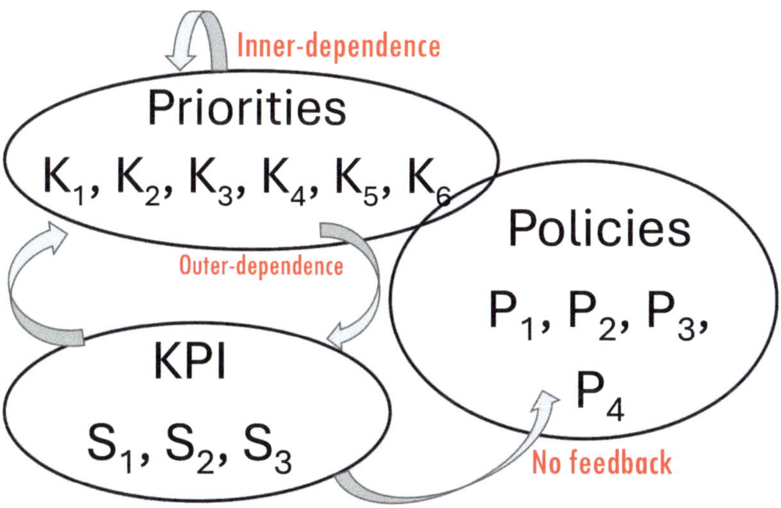

Fig. 6.3 Framework of survey questionnaires. *Source*: Author's construction

The choice of all those elements was based on the pre-survey dialogues we conducted prior to the survey with some bankers and analysts to ensure that the survey framework and the questionnaires captured the real conditions on the ground. Although the elements in Priorities and those in KPI are mutually exclusive, some of them are interrelated (outer dependence). We also learned that some elements within Priorities are interrelated (the case of inner dependence); see Fig. 6.3. Given these interdependencies, we made an attempt to ensure that the model used in the survey incorporates them explicitly to avoid misrepresentation.

In the tradition of Bayesian approach, a better outcome of any decision-making problem is obtained by combining statistical data together with the cause-and-effect relationships. Therefore, for our survey, a model capable of capturing the nature and intensity of dependencies between the KPI and the Priorities is preferred. Respondents will have more choices by using a diversity of information to reflect those dependencies. Specifically, we used the Analytical Network Process (ANP) approach to capture the details and accuracy of the respondents' judgments and represent them in a reliable mathematical framework. To the extent the diverse information are not restricted to the finding of new experiments or any statistical test concerned with probabilities, the approach is rather different than that represented by Bayes' theorem (which is considered as a special case of ANP). For the network in ANP to have entries of the vectors as limiting priorities, Bayesian theory is a sufficient but not a necessary condition.[3]

[3] As a general theory of relative measurement, ANP is used to derive composite priority ratio scales from individual ratio scales, capturing the outcome of dependence and feedback within and between clusters of elements. Each priority scale reflects the relative importance of the elements in

Fig. 6.4 Super-matrix W with elements of KPI and priorities. *Source*: Author's construction

$$
\begin{array}{c|cc}
 & \text{KPI (3)} & \text{Priorities (6)} \\
\hline
\begin{array}{c}\text{KPI (3)}\\ \text{n, r, q}\end{array} & 0 & \alpha W_{12} \\
\begin{array}{c}\text{Priorities (6)}\\ \text{m, i, j}\end{array} & \varepsilon W_{21} & \beta W_{22}
\end{array}
$$

A key question is what will guarantee the reliability of that information? The knowledge and experience of the respondents will be the one, although we are fully aware that the respondents may be bias. Their cognitive shortcuts or tendencies (biases) can affect their judgments and conclusions. Hence, in designing the questionnaires and conducting the interviews, we need to emphasize the importance of minimizing bias-related risks.[4] In synthesizing the responses' judgments, we used the concept of dominance, expressed through importance, preference, and likelihood as the counterpart of probabilities in the Bayesian approach.

What we wish to find out is the relative importance of liquidity preference by the bank (relative to the other two KPI elements). This is derived from the priority ranking of KPI after taking into account the relative importance of elements in Priorities. The inclusion of Policies cluster is intended for policy recommendations after we have the priority ranking of KPI and the ranking of Policies elements under each of the KPI elements. Since there is no interdependence of elements in Policies and those in KPI and Priorities, the priority ranking of Policies is obtained by using matrix multiplication technique typically used in the AHP.

To find the priority ranking of the KPI elements, the following supermatrix W is used containing all the elements of KPI and Priorities (Fig. 6.4), where W_{12} is the weighted matrix of KPI given each element of Priorities. It represents the probabilities of the 'KPI' causing a given set of 'Priorities'. W_{21} is the weighted matrix of priorities for each element of the KPI. It represents the matrix of relative importance, importance or presence of 'Priorities' given KPI.[5] W_{22} is the weighted matrix of Priorities under each element of Priorities (within-group pairwise com-

the system. This relative importance is affected by some constraints and boundaries called limiting priorities (see Saaty, 2010).

[4] There are numerous types of human biases, ranging from status quo bias (preferring things to stay the same and resisting change), anchoring bias (relying too heavily on the first piece of information), confirmation bias (tend to use information in a way that confirms one's preexisting beliefs), hindsight bias (believing to have accurate prediction after an event has occurred), to self-serving bias (attributing negative outcomes to external factors and positive outcomes to one's own actions). During interviews, we also paid particular attention to the risks of another bias, i.e. people tend to have the same perceptions (in line) as those belonging to the same group (in-group bias).

[5] Note that W12 and W21 can be estimated either through some statistical techniques or through respondent judgments. Using statistical techniques, W_{12} corresponds to the posteriors of W_{21}.

parisons).[6] It represents the matrix of interrelations among the 'Priorities' estimated through judgments. Probabilistically, W_{22} gives the likelihood that given an element of 'Priorities' the other elements of 'Priorities' are also present (they are observed in a given respondent). From matrix W one can derive the priorities or likelihoods of the 'KPI' given the 'Priorities'.

The detailed procedures and steps to capture the perceptions and priority ranking of the respondents along with a brief mathematical exposition of the ANP theory are presented in Appendix 6.1. In order to compare the impact of the collection of clusters and elements of Priorities and KPI, that is, obtaining a vector of weights in a pairwise comparison matrix, we need to make the supermatrix column stochastic. Since individually blocks W_{12},W_{22}, and W_{21} contain the weights of elements within each corresponding cluster, each of them is column stochastic, the supermatrix combining them shown in Fig. 6.4 is not column stochastic. Hence, we need to also weigh the impacts of the clusters on each cluster in a pairwise comparison matrix to obtain a vector of weights for the column of those clusters. The corresponding question to ask is: Which of the two clusters has the greater influence on a given cluster?

Since treating interconnectedness in an explicit way is crucial for accurately capturing the dependencies and feedback among elements in the network, we need to make the supermatrix W irreducible where every element in the network can be influenced by every other element (directly or indirectly). Having W irreducible, the computation of limiting priorities is guaranteed to reflect the true nature of the interdependencies and feedback among all elements in the network.[7] Since matrix W is irreducible, the resulting weighted supermatrix is also irreducible. The limiting priorities of W are obtained by solving the following eigenvalue problem:

$$\begin{pmatrix} 0 & \alpha_1 W_{12} \\ W_{21} & \alpha_2 W_{22} \end{pmatrix} \begin{pmatrix} w_1 \\ w_2 \end{pmatrix} = \begin{pmatrix} w_1 \\ w_2 \end{pmatrix}$$

the solution of which is given by:

$$w_2 = \left[\lim_{k \to \infty} (\alpha_1 W_{21} W_{12} + \alpha_2 W_{22})^k \right] e,$$

$$e = (1, \ldots, 1)^T,$$

$$w_1 = \alpha_1 W_{12} w_2.$$

[6] Super matrix is a matrix of matrices, representing the relationships and influences among various elements and clusters, where each element within it has its own priority scale.

[7] An irreducible matrix is a square matrix where its rows and columns cannot be rearranged to isolate smaller submatrices along the diagonal. If a supermatrix is reducible, some clusters may be isolated or not properly linked with others. In such a case, the influences and dependencies within the network can be inaccurately represented, and the resulting limiting priorities can be incorrect or misleading.

Since there are no dependencies among the 'priorities', $W_{22} = 0$. In Bayes' theorem, the terms w_1 are the vector of prior probabilities of the 'KPI' and w_2 is the vector of likelihoods of the 'Priorities'. The final outcome

$$\begin{pmatrix} w_1 \\ w_2 \end{pmatrix}$$

which is the set of priorities or likelihoods of all elements and clusters including the relative preference for liquidity in KPI, is obtained by raising the supermatrix W multiple (k) times to power until the result of the iterations is converged (see again Appendix 6.1). With those vectors of priorities, we could then focus on finding the ranking of the course of action (Policies). Note that since the respondents in the survey are local banks, the relative preference for liquidity derived from the model reflects the behavior of local banks, which plays a central role in the analysis of monetary policy effect based on the behavioral approach.

6.2.2 Survey Results

The results presented in this Section are based on the survey conducted by using the above model framework. The respondents consist of banks, classified into state-owned banks, private banks, people's credit bank (*Bank Perekonomian Rakyat*, BPR) and regional development bank (*Bank Pembangunan Daerah*, BPD). The field survey was conducted over the period of June to October 2025.

As described earlier, we broke down the problem into 3 clusters or components: Priorities consist of 6 elements (K1....K6), Key Performance Indicators or KPI consist of 3 elements (S1, S2, and S3), and Policies consist of 4 elements (P1... P4). What is shown in Table 6.1 is an example of the limiting supermatrix W for a private bank in Yogyakarta. The unweighted supermatrix and the weighted one are shown in Appendix 6.2. The bottom part of the limiting supermatrix shows the relative importance of each element in the priorities. The ranking shows that extending regular credit (receiving 0.206) and accumulating regular saving (0.205) are ranked as the top two, and the least prioritized is making Sharia placement (0.053). Upon checking the balance sheets of other private banks in Yogyakarta and looking at the loan-to-deposit ratio discussed earlier, it is true that they hold a lot more deposits than credits, and this may have prompted their preference toward allocating more credit.

But such priority preferences are not independent of the KPI of the banks. Since our main goal is to evaluate the relative importance of liquidity preference, we asked direct questions about it. That led them to rank the preferences towards KPI. Obviously, a different ranking of KPI would imply a different ranking of Priorities. The KPI ranking, shown in the upper part of the supermatrix, shows that the bank's liquidity preference is the highest (0.119), followed by profitability (0.117) and solvability (0.097). Hence, the data showing the low loan-to-deposit ratio in the

Table 6.1 Limiting supermatrix: the case of private bank in Yogyakarta

	Liquidity	Profit	Solvability	Regular credit	Regular placements	Regular savings	Sharia credits	Sharia placements	Sharia savings
Liquidity	0.11873	0.11873	0.11873	0.11873	0.11873	0.11873	0.11873	0.11873	0.11873
Profit	0.1174	0.1174	0.1174	0.1174	0.1174	0.1174	0.1174	0.1174	0.1174
Solvability	0.0972	0.0972	0.0972	0.0972	0.0972	0.0972	0.0972	0.0972	0.0972
Regular credit	0.20646	0.20646	0.20646	0.20646	0.20646	0.20646	0.20646	0.20646	0.20646
Regular placement	0.08984	0.08984	0.08984	0.08984	0.08984	0.08984	0.08984	0.08984	0.08984
Regular savings	0.205	0.205	0.205	0.205	0.205	0.205	0.205	0.205	0.205
Sharia credits	0.05624	0.05624	0.05624	0.05624	0.05624	0.05624	0.05624	0.05624	0.05624
Sharia placements	0.05331	0.05331	0.05331	0.05331	0.05331	0.05331	0.05331	0.05331	0.05331
Sharia savings	0.05581	0.05581	0.05581	0.05581	0.05581	0.05581	0.05581	0.05581	0.05581

Source: Results of applying the limiting supermatrix to questionnaires for a local private bank in Yogyakarta

Table 6.2 Geometric mean of survey results (The case of local banks in Yogyakarta)

Geometric mean calculations for avg. ranking			
Banks in Yogya (Java)			
	S1	S2	S3
State-owned bank	0.173174	0.118844	0.041316
Local government bank	0.200364	0.090545	0.042425
BPR	0.127365	0.116311	0.089658
Private bank	0.118732	0.117402	0.097199
Geometric mean	0.151349178	0.11009287	0.062516944
	0.46717697	0.339848896	0.192974134

Notes: S1 = Liquidity; S2 = Profitability; S3 = Solvency
Source: Results of the survey

region are aligned with what the bank perceived during the survey, i.e., the high liquidity preference.

Collecting the survey results from all 4 categories of banks and applying the geometric mean, the final ranking is shown in Table 6.2. Notice that the ranking is the same regardless of the bank category: liquidity (S1) first, followed by profitability (S2) and solvency (S3). The bottom row of the table shows the geometric mean before and after normalization. Clearly, banks in Yogyakarta have a high liquidity preference.

Upon further discussion with other bankers in the region, a number of reasons why liquidity was the most important for them were mentioned. One is the regulatory requirement on the reserve that banks have to maintain at Bank Indonesia.[8] At the time of the survey, the requirement was 9%. This regulation is meant to ensure that banks have enough liquidity to meet their obligations and to help maintain financial stability. That 9% ratio of reserves requirement, imposed since September 2022 when COVID-19 was already less severe, was almost double compared to the ratio few years back; e.g., 5.0% in 2022. In effect, these reserves determine how much cash banks must hold versus how much they can lend. The higher the requirement rate, the lower the amount of funds available for lending.

On the demand side, it is important to note that at the time of the survey the economy was not fully stabilized yet. The rebound was uneven and sluggish. The high economic uncertainties at the time cast a shadow over the recovery process, forcing business communities to exercise financial caution. Non-performing loans (NPL) also increased quite dramatically in some banks, because many businesses faced great difficulties during the pandemic.[9] All these strengthened banks' pref-

[8] The reserve requirement for sharia banks and sharia business units is slightly lower, i.e., 7.5%.

[9] This was despite the fact that the government had tried to help businesses, including micro, small, and medium enterprises (MSMEs), through various programs such as tax relief (corporate tax rate was reduced from 25 to 20%), loan moratoriums, debt forgiveness, interest rate subsidies, and grants provision. At the national budget level, the government also allowed for a budget deficit limit to exceed 3% of GDP, mandatory spending to be more flexibly adjusted, and the

erence to keep liquidity high as part of their risk management. Most banks turned to be more conservative with their lending strategy, among others, by maintaining higher cash reserves.

Extending the coverage of the loan-to-deposit ratio to include all banks in Jawa, the average ratio is less-than 100% (see again Fig. 6.2). Assuming that the ratio is aligned with what banks actually prefer, we can surmise that, in general, the banks in Jawa have a strong liquidity preference. Since by any measure Jawa banks dominate the nation's banking system, one could deduce that the Indonesian overall banking system has a relatively high liquidity preference and the loan size is smaller than the deposit (at the time of writing, the country's loan-to-deposit ratio was 87%).

The results of the survey for banks outside Jawa varied. As an example, Tables 6.3 and 6.4 show the supermatrices of a state-owned bank and a BPR in Sorong, Papua Barat. In the case of a state-owned bank, the preference for liquidity was clearly expressed (0.15), followed by profitability (0.12), and solvability (0.07). However, BPR in that region put profitability (0.16) in a higher position than liquidity (0.11).

During in-depth discussions, it was revealed that many BPR in that region were concerned about their liquidity position. They had to monitor and make rather frequent adjustments to their strategies, including offering incentives and enticing interest rates on deposits. They were also more short-term oriented as a large portion of their credit had shorter maturities. In the case of state-owned banks, they were more aiming at profits and engaged in aggressive lending by offering competitive loan products to attract greater number of clients. In an effort to increase their loan portfolios and interest income, they also focused on reducing operational costs to improve their profit margins. This was done, among others, by adopting digital technology, albeit only for some operational tasks. Through customer segmentation, they targeted high-value customers who could generate more revenue. They were also active in marketing and sales efforts, offering various types of promotions and incentives and wanted to offer a wide range of financial products and services to meet different customer needs. All of these efforts were aimed at maximizing bank revenue streams. Internally, bank employees and managers were often evaluated based on performance criteria related to loan growth and sales target.

Other banks that put profitability above liquidity indicated that they adopted a similar approach. This was also the case for other banks in Papua-Barat as well as banks in other regions outside of Jawa covered in our survey (e.g., Nusa Tenggara Timur, Maluku, North Sumatera and Aceh). Among them, they shared one common thing: having fewer problems with liquidity and are more concerned with revenue.

issuance of government bonds to increase, of which Bank Indonesia was the largest buyer. More recently, another debt forgiveness program for MSMEs, especially those operating in agriculture and fisheries was introduced through Government Regulation No. 47 of 2024. Borrowers unable to repay 10-year loans (a cap of Rp300 million for individuals and a cap of Rp500 million for business entities) are eligible for the program. Some individual banks also introduced their program unilaterally, for example, the debt write-off program by Bank Mandiri.

Table 6.3 Limiting supermatrix: the case of state-owned bank in Sorong, Papua Barat

	Liquidity	Profit	Solvabity	Regular credit	Regular placements	Regular savings	Sharia credits	Sharia placements	Sharia savings
Liquidity	0.14669	0.14669	0.14669	0.14669	0.14669	0.14669	0.14669	0.14669	0.14669
Profit	0.12039	0.12039	0.12039	0.12039	0.12039	0.12039	0.12039	0.12039	0.12039
Solvability	0.06625	0.06625	0.06625	0.06625	0.06625	0.06625	0.06625	0.06625	0.06625
Regular credit	0.21026	0.21026	0.21026	0.21026	0.21026	0.21026	0.21026	0.21026	0.21026
Regular placement	0.23038	0.23038	0.23038	0.23038	0.23038	0.23038	0.23038	0.23038	0.23038
Regular savings	0.12525	0.12525	0.12525	0.12525	0.12525	0.12525	0.12525	0.12525	0.12525
Sharia credits	0.03315	0.03315	0.03315	0.03315	0.03315	0.03315	0.03315	0.03315	0.03315
Sharia placements	0.03509	0.03509	0.03509	0.03509	0.03509	0.03509	0.03509	0.03509	0.03509
Sharia savings	0.03254	0.03254	0.03254	0.03254	0.03254	0.03254	0.03254	0.03254	0.03254

Source: Results of the survey

Table 6.4 Limiting supermatrix: the case of BPR in Sorong, Papua Barat

	Liquidity	Profit	Solvabity	Regular credit	Regular placements	Regular savings	Sharia credits	Sharia placements	Sharia savings
Liquidity	0.10839	0.10839	0.10839	0.10839	0.10839	0.10839	0.10839	0.10839	0.10839
Profit	0.15788	0.15788	0.15788	0.15788	0.15788	0.15788	0.15788	0.15788	0.15788
Solvabity	0.06706	0.06706	0.06706	0.06706	0.06706	0.06706	0.06706	0.06706	0.06706
Regular credit	0.18493	0.18493	0.18493	0.18493	0.18493	0.18493	0.18493	0.18493	0.18493
Regular placement	0.21218	0.21218	0.21218	0.21218	0.21218	0.21218	0.21218	0.21218	0.21218
Regular savings	0.18499	0.18499	0.18499	0.18499	0.18499	0.18499	0.18499	0.18499	0.18499
Sharia credits	0.02813	0.02813	0.02813	0.02813	0.02813	0.02813	0.02813	0.02813	0.02813
Sharia placements	0.02822	0.02822	0.02822	0.02822	0.02822	0.02822	0.02822	0.02822	0.02822
Sharia savings	0.02822	0.02822	0.02822	0.02822	0.02822	0.02822	0.02822	0.02822	0.02822

Source: Results of the survey

Table 6.5 Priority ranking of banks in Jawa and Non-Jawa

	Jawa	Non-Jawa
State-own banks	S1 >S2 >S3	S2 >S1 >S3
Private banks	S1 >S2 >S3	S1 >S2 >S3
BPR	S1 >S2 >S3	S2 >S1 >S3
BPD	S1 >S2 >S3	S2 >S1 >S3

Notes: S1 = Liquidity; S2 = Profitability; S3 = Solvency
Source: Results of the survey

Examples of the limiting supermatrices for state-owned banks in these regions are shown in Appendix 6.3.

To the extent many banks in Jawa (and also some private banks outside Jawa) have more investment options, they can allocate the deposit fund for assets other than credit such as government bonds, equity, securities. They tend to be more proactive and aggressive in expanding their depositor base. Hence, their liquidity preference is generally stronger than that of smaller banks or those operating outside Jawa. Since the financial market is more limited and narrower in the latter, a large share of assets are allocated for credit. The only non-credit option they have is to put the money in other banks (interbank placement) in the form of saving or demand deposits just to earn some returns. This conforms with the data on loan-to-deposit ratio discussed earlier, where in average credit issued by banks outside Jawa is greater than their deposit, while in Jawa it is the opposite.

In summary, Table 6.5 shows the average results of the priority ranking for the KPI of the banks in Jawa and Non-Jawa. As is clearly seen,

Although this conclusion is important for analyzing the impact of monetary policy, particularly on regional development (structural versus behavior approach) and also for evaluating the effectiveness of the policy, it is also clear that the loan-to-deposit ratio does not always provide the right guidance for detecting bank liquidity preference. There are banks that keep a high loan-to-deposit ratio but express to have a strong liquidity preference as their KPI, and there are banks with a low ratio and yet their operations are said to be guided by the preference towards profitability more than liquidity. In other words, the data do not always align with their perceptions. Table 6.6 summarizes the cases where the loan-to-deposit ratio aligns with their preference toward liquidity and where it is not.

Given what the local banks perceived toward their Priorities and KPI, what would be the policies or the course of actions they prefer to have. Following the method described in the preceding Section, the survey results show that different types of bank have different preferences. Heterogeneous preferences are also found across regions. In Yogyakarta, the state-owned banks and the BPR felt that improving their own internal governance is the most needed course of action, while the BPD and the private bank considered that the loosening of some regulations should be prioritized. The latter was also expressed by BPD in Ambon and Aceh and by BPR in Ambon, Kupang, Sorong, and Aceh. Meanwhile, BPD prioritized improving the

Table 6.6 Alignment between loan to deposit ratio and the survey results

	Survey	LDR	Aligned
Yogyakarta			
Private banks	S1 > S2 > S3	Liquidity	Yes
State-own banks	S1 > S2 > S3	Liquidity	Yes
BPR	S1 > S2 > S3	Profitability	No
BPD	S1 > S2 > S3	Liquidity	Yes
Aceh			
Bank Syariah	S1 >S2 >S3	Liquidity	Yes
Private Syariah	S1 >S2 >S3	Liquidity	Yes
BPRS Syariah	S2 >S1 >S3	Liquidity	No
North Sumatera			
Private banks	S1 >S2 >S3	Liquidity	Yes
State-own banks	S2 >S1 >S3	Profitability	Yes
BPR	S2 >S1 >S3	Profitability	Yes
BPD	S2 >S1 >S3	Profitability	Yes
Maluku (North)			
State-own banks	S2 >S1 >S3	Liquidity	No
BPR	S1 >S2 >S3	Liquidity	Yes
BPD	S2 >S1 >S3	Profitability	Yes
East Nusa Tenggara			
State-own banks	S2 >S1 >S3	Liquidity	No
BPR	S2 >S1 >S3	Profitability	Yes
BPD	S2 >S1 >S3	Profitability	Yes
Papua (West)			
State-own banks	S1 >S2 >S3	Liquidity	Yes
BPR	S1 >S2 >S3	Liquidity	No
BPD	S2 >S1 >S3	Liquidity	No

Source: Processed from the survey and BPS Statistik Ekonomi dan Keuangan Daerah (various series)

internal governance of the bank in Kupang and Sorong, and by state-owned banks and BPR in Medan (North Sumatera).

Taking the geometric mean, the overall results for the whole country show that improving governance is the top priority for BPD and BPR, while for state-owned banks and private banks, the adoption / improvement of digital technology is the most needed course of action (Fig. 6.5). The complete set of the results for each region / bank surveyed is available upon request.

The governance problems cited are often related to poor risk management of the bank (which can cause high nonperforming loans, NPL) and the lack of internal controls needed to detect and prevent irregularities. This is due, among others, to a limited quality of human resources (a lack of necessary skills and training) that could result in mismanagement and poor performance. BPRs are particularly vulnerable to such conditions. Some of them had a low degree of compliance with

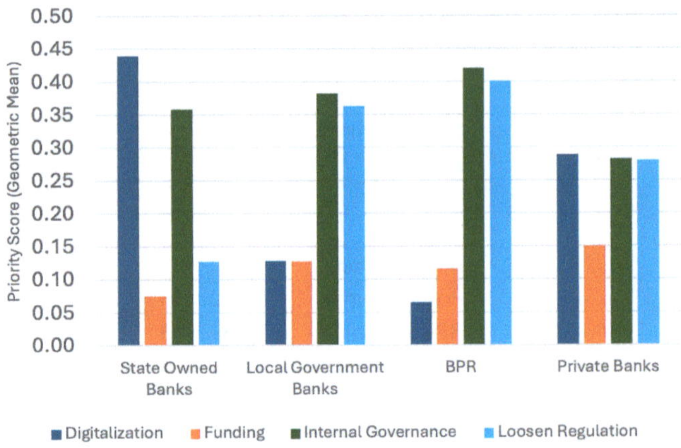

Fig. 6.5 The priority ranking of policies (course of actions). *Source*: Results of the survey (the geometric mean)

regulatory requirements, leading to significant financial losses, legal-cum-financial penalties, and a lack of trust among customers. In some cases, the main reason was simply fraud and corruption, or they had a lack of transparency in financial reporting and decision-making processes. During in-depth discussions, we also encountered cases of conflict-of-interest due to the ownership structure of the bank.

Despite these predicaments, most of them were of the opinion that improving bank governance can be a powerful tool to mitigate liquidity problems. Implementing more robust risk management frameworks, such as better monitoring of loan quality and deposit stability, improving transparency and timely reporting, and improving the roles and responsibilities of bank boards and senior management in overseeing liquidity risk management, were examples cited by those we interviewed. In less developed regions outside Jawa, some banks also highlighted the importance of promoting financial education, especially for the low-income population and small and medium enterprises (SMEs). They constitute the largest share of their customers. They also believed that policies to promote financial inclusion can help increase the stability of deposits and reduce liquidity risks.

Several banks, particularly BPR, expressed regulatory problems with respect to the minimum paid-up capital requirement. Currently, there are more than 1000 BPR, and almost all of their clients are MSME. This suggests that they could play a strategic role in the promotion of millions of small businesses throughout the country. According to the new regulation mandated by the P2SK Law (regarding the Development and Strengthening of the Financial Sector), the paid-up capital for BPR is set according to the designated zone: i.e., for Zone 1 it is IDR 6 billion, for Zone 2 it is IDR 4 billion, and for Zone 3 the minimum amount is IDR 2 billion. This is considered a significant burden for smaller banks. The regulation also includes provisions for mergers and consolidations for BPRs owned and/or controlled by the same Controlling Shareholders within a single main island or archipelagic region.[10]

Appendix 6.1: Step-by-Step Procedure to Derive the Priorities of KPI and Policies

Step A There are 6 priorities ($K_1, \ldots, K_6$). We rank the 6 priorities with respect to each of them. For example, given the extension of regular credit as Priority (K_3), which other Priorities are most relevant or most important to have in order to achieve K_3. This leads to a pairwise comparison matrix of 6 by 6 from which we can derive the eigen vector β. Since there are 6 priorities, we will have 6 of these matrices and 6 eigen vectors, $\beta_1, \ldots, \beta_6$. This will be the entries of the submatrix βW_{22} (see again Fig. 6.4).

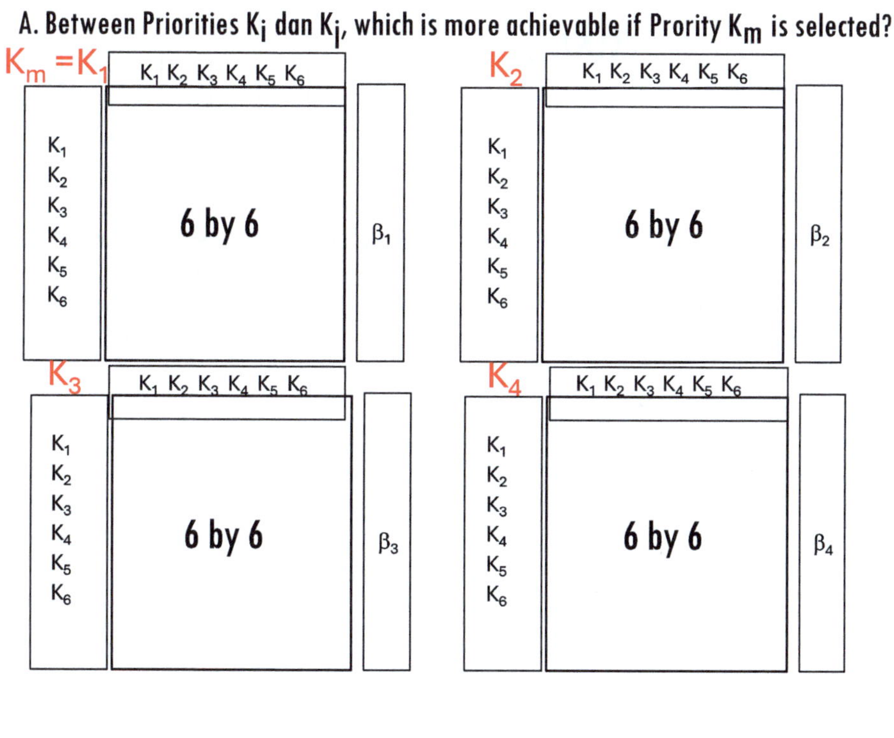

[10] Other regulations include the requirement for BPRs or Sharia BPRs owned and/or controlled by the same Controlling Shareholders within a single main island or archipelagic region to undergo consolidation through a merger within a maximum of 2 years (3 years for regional government-owned BPRs or Sharia BPRs). They must also complete nomenclature changes in 2 years (Deloitte, 2024).

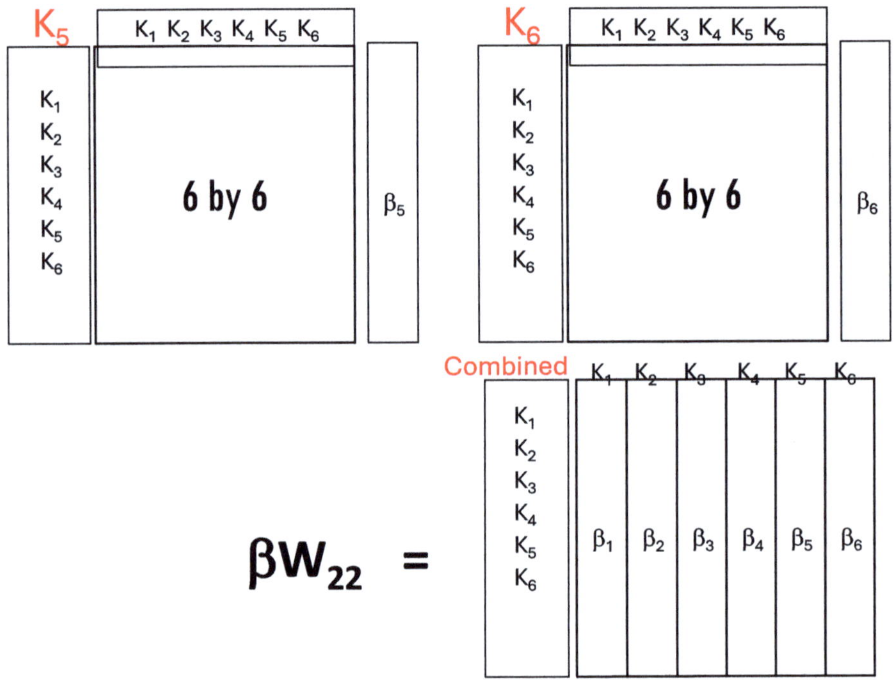

Step B Next, we rank the Priorities for a given KPI. Since there are 3 KPI (S_1, S_2, S_3) and six priorities, we will have three pairwise comparison matrices, each of the size of 6-by-6, and three eigen vectors γ_1, γ_2, γ_3. This gives us a matrix of 6 by 3 as shown in the 'Combined' matrix above, the entries of which will enter the submatrix εW_{21}

B. If KPI S_n, is selected, which Priority is more achievable/relevant, K_i or K_j?

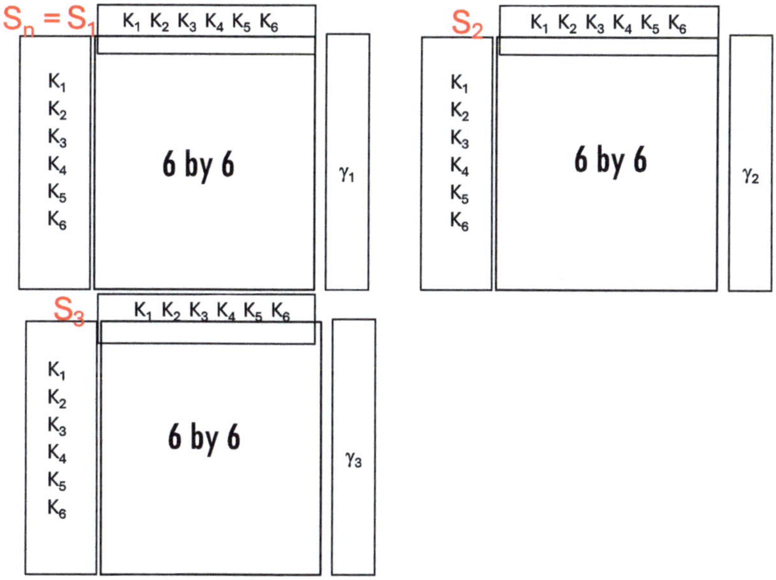

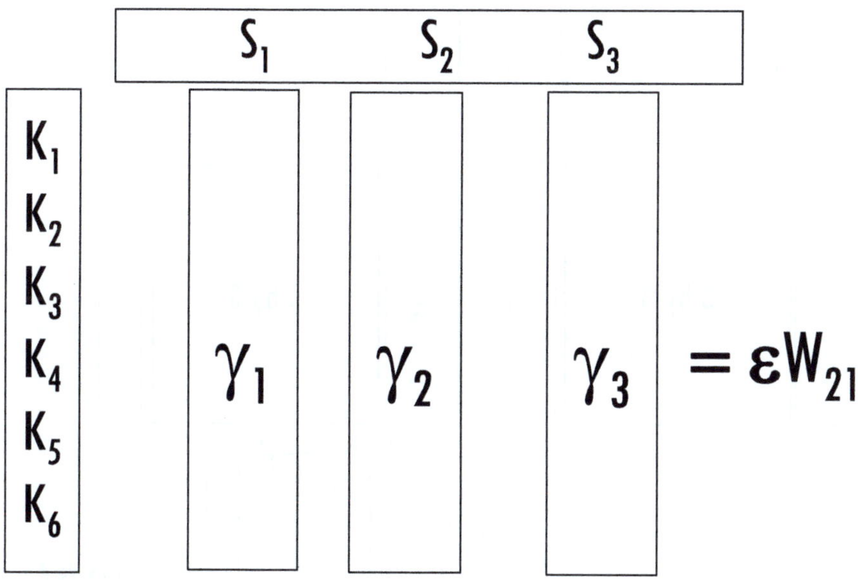

Step C Our main goal here is to find the KPI priorities. This is done by ranking the KPI given each of the Priorities, giving us six of 3-by-3 pairwise comparison matrices, and six eigen vectors $\alpha 1 \ldots\ldots \alpha 6$. Rearranging, we will have a 3-by-6 matrix that shows the ranking of KPI under each Priorities (see the last matrix below).

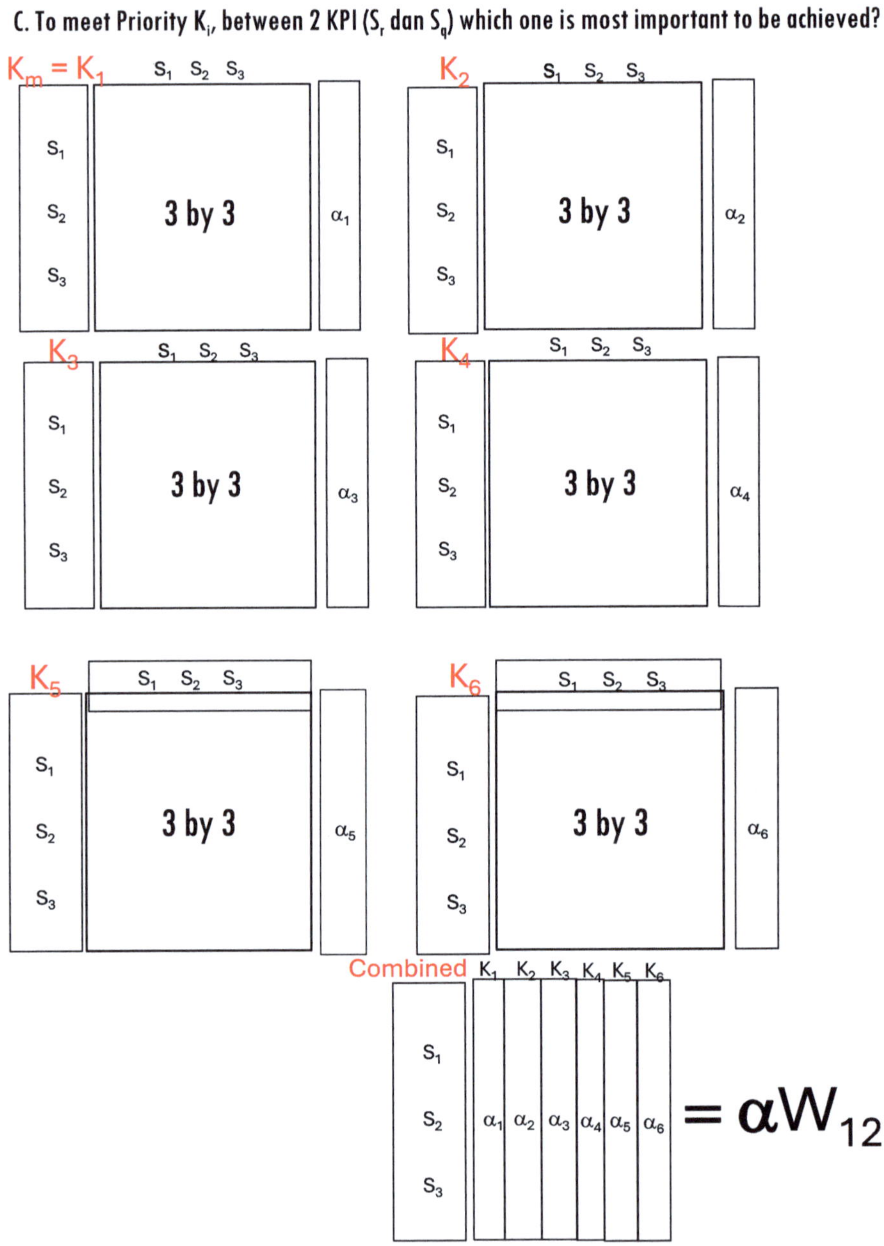

Now that we have a set of matrices, i.e., 6-by-6, 6-by-3, and 3-by-6, we form a 9-by-9 supermatrix. This is called the uneweighted supermatrix, which is nonstochastic. To guarantee that the resulting priorities reflect the true nature of the interdependencies and feedback among all elements in the network, we need to make this supermatrix irreducible, where every element in the network can be influenced by every other element (directly or indirectly).

What we need to do next is to transform this unweighted supermatrix into a weighted supermatrix that is column stochastic. Since the unweighted supermatrix is irreducible, the weighted supermatrix is also irreducible. An example of a unweighted and weighted supermatrix for Yogyakarta case is shown in Appendix 6.2. The final supermatrix, called the limiting supermatrix, is obtained by raising the weighted supermatrix multiple times (k) to power until the result of the iterations converges. This gives us the final results of the computation. An example of a supermatrix limitation for a private bank in Yogyakarta is shown in Table 6.1 in the text. The limiting supermatrix for state-owned banks in other regions is shown in Appendix 6.3.

Step D Let us denote the vector of the final classification of the KPI by V_{KPI}. To find the best course of action, given the final ranking of the KPI and the prioritizations, we apply the *Analytic Hierarchy Process (AHP)* approach by first classifying the priorities for the four policies, P_1, P_2, P_3, P_4 under each of the KPIs.

Hence, we will have three pairwise comparison matrices each of size 4×4, from which we generate three eigen vectors, μ_1, μ_2, μ_3. Arrange them into a matrix of 4×3 and multiply it by V_{KPI} will give us the ranking of the Policies P_1^*, P_2^*, P_3^*, P_4^* (see matrix multiplication at the bottom):

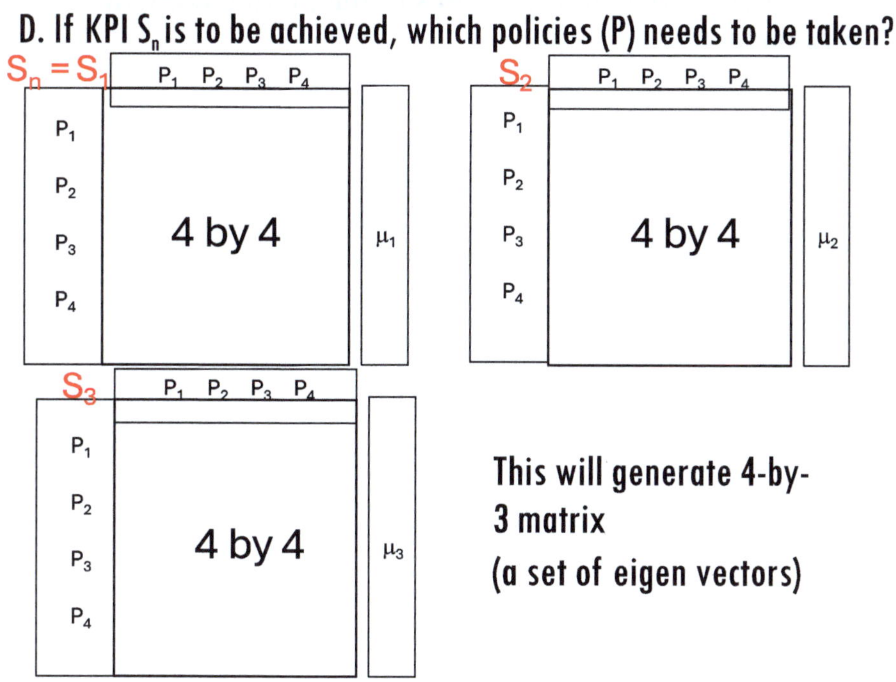

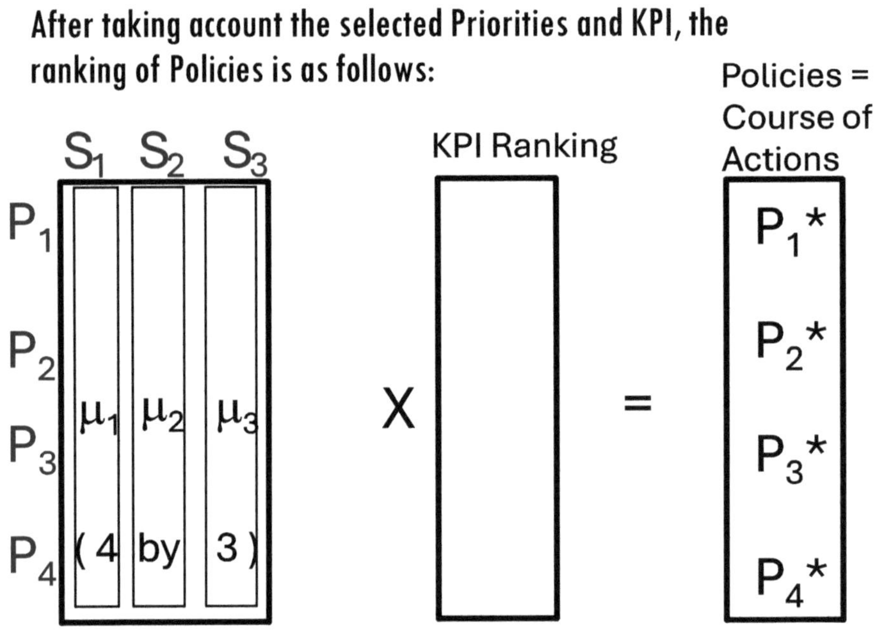

Appendix 6.2: Unweighted Supermatrix and Weighted Supermatrix of the Survey Results of the Private Bank in Yogyakarta

Unweighted Supermatrix

Unweighted SM	Liquidity	Profit	Solvability	Regular credit	Regular placements	Regular savings	Sharia credits	Sharia placements	Sharia savings
Liquidity	0	0	0	0.08414	0.08096	0.76924	0.33333	0.33333	0.33333
Profit	0	0	0	0.70494	0.18839	0.084	0.33333	0.33333	0.33333
Solvability	0	0	0	0.21092	0.73064	0.14676	0.33333	0.33333	0.33333
Regular credit	0.28496	0.51985	0.29607	0.43071	0.16667	0.16667	0.16667	0.16667	0.16667
Regular placement	0.11344	0.12024	0.11826	0.12025	0.16667	0.16667	0.16667	0.16667	0.16667
Regular savings	0.48819	0.24815	0.47212	0.32615	0.16667	0.16667	0.16667	0.16667	0.16667
Sharia credits	0.03622	0.04127	0.03805	0.04885	0.16667	0.16667	0.16667	0.16667	0.16667
Sharia placements	0.03342	0.03404	0.03387	0.03587	0.16667	0.16667	0.16667	0.16667	0.16667
Sharia savings	0.04376	0.03645	0.04163	0.03817	0.16667	0.16667	0.16667	0.16667	0.16667

Weighted Supermatrix

Weighted SM	Liquidity	Profit	Solvability	Regular credit	Regular placements	Regular savings	Sharia credits	Sharia placements	Sharia savings
Liquidity	0	0	0	0.04207	0.04048	0.38462	0.16667	0.16667	0.16667
Profit	0	0	0	0.35247	0.0942	0.042	0.16667	0.16667	0.16667
Solvability	0	0	0	0.10546	0.36532	0.07338	0.16667	0.16667	0.16667
Regular credit	0.28496	0.51985	0.29607	0.21535	0.08333	0.08333	0.08333	0.08333	0.08333
Regular placement	0.11344	0.12024	0.11826	0.16013	0.08333	0.08333	0.08333	0.08333	0.08333
Regular savings	0.48819	0.24815	0.47212	0.16307	0.08333	0.08333	0.08333	0.08333	0.08333
Sharia credits	0.03622	0.04127	0.03805	0.02442	0.08333	0.08333	0.08333	0.08333	0.08333
Sharia placements	0.03342	0.03404	0.03387	0.03787	0.08333	0.08333	0.08333	0.08333	0.08333
Sharia savings	0.04376	0.03645	0.04163	0.01908	0.08333	0.08333	0.08333	0.08333	0.08333

Appendix 6.3: Limiting Supermatrix of the Survey Results for State-Owned Banks in Various Regions

Aceh: Local State Bank

Limit SM	Liquidity	Profit	Solvability	Regular credit	Regular placements	Regular savings	Sharia credits	Sharia placements	Sharia savings
Liquidity	0.1386	0.1386	0.1386	0.1386	0.1386	0.1386	0.1386	0.1386	0.1386
Profit	0.13763	0.13763	0.13763	0.13763	0.13763	0.13763	0.13763	0.13763	0.13763
Solvability	0.05711	0.05711	0.05711	0.05711	0.05711	0.05711	0.05711	0.05711	0.05711
Regular credit	0.021	0.021	0.021	0.021	0.021	0.021	0.021	0.021	0.021
Regular placement	0.02529	0.02529	0.02529	0.02529	0.02529	0.02529	0.02529	0.02529	0.02529
Regular savings	0.02175	0.02175	0.02175	0.02175	0.02175	0.02175	0.02175	0.02175	0.02175
Sharia credits	0.27518	0.27518	0.27518	0.27518	0.27518	0.27518	0.27518	0.27518	0.27518
Sharia placements	0.11341	0.11341	0.11341	0.11341	0.11341	0.11341	0.11341	0.11341	0.11341
Sharia savings	0.21004	0.21004	0.21004	0.21004	0.21004	0.21004	0.21004	0.21004	0.21004

Medan: North Sumatera

Limit SM	Liquidity	Profit	Solvability	Regular credit	Regular placements	Regular savings	Sharia credits	Sharia placements	Sharia savings
Liquidity	0.1062	0.1062	0.1062	0.1062	0.1062	0.1062	0.1062	0.1062	0.1062
Profit	0.13384	0.13384	0.13384	0.13384	0.13384	0.13384	0.13384	0.13384	0.13384
Solvability	0.0933	0.0933	0.0933	0.0933	0.0933	0.0933	0.0933	0.0933	0.0933
Regular credit	0.24376	0.24376	0.24376	0.24376	0.24376	0.24376	0.24376	0.24376	0.24376
Regular placement	0.14685	0.14685	0.14685	0.14685	0.14685	0.14685	0.14685	0.14685	0.14685
Regular savings	0.18581	0.18581	0.18581	0.18581	0.18581	0.18581	0.18581	0.18581	0.18581
Sharia credits	0.03116	0.03116	0.03116	0.03116	0.03116	0.03116	0.03116	0.03116	0.03116
Sharia placements	0.02955	0.02955	0.02955	0.02955	0.02955	0.02955	0.02955	0.02955	0.02955
Sharia savings	0.02955	0.02955	0.02955	0.02955	0.02955	0.02955	0.02955	0.02955	0.02955

Kupang: NTT

Limit SM	Liquidity	Profit	Solvability	Regular credit	Regular placements	Regular savings	Sharia credits	Sharia placements	Sharia savings
Liquidity	0.10086	0.10086	0.10086	0.10086	0.10086	0.10086	0.10086	0.10086	0.10086
Profit	0.15758	0.15758	0.15758	0.15758	0.15758	0.15758	0.15758	0.15758	0.15758
Solvability	0.07489	0.07489	0.07489	0.07489	0.07489	0.07489	0.07489	0.07489	0.07489
Regular credit	0.23475	0.23475	0.23475	0.23475	0.23475	0.23475	0.23475	0.23475	0.23475
Regular placement	0.15222	0.15222	0.15222	0.15222	0.15222	0.15222	0.15222	0.15222	0.15222
Regular savings	0.18178	0.18178	0.18178	0.18178	0.18178	0.18178	0.18178	0.18178	0.18178
Sharia credits	0.03326	0.03326	0.03326	0.03326	0.03326	0.03326	0.03326	0.03326	0.03326
Sharia placements	0.03247	0.03247	0.03247	0.03247	0.03247	0.03247	0.03247	0.03247	0.03247
Sharia savings	0.03219	0.03219	0.03219	0.03219	0.03219	0.03219	0.03219	0.03219	0.03219

Ambon: Maluku

Limit SM	Liquidity	Profit	Solvability	Regular credit	Regular placements	Regular savings	Sharia credits	Sharia placements	Sharia savings
Liquidity	0.10445	0.10445	0.10445	0.10445	0.10445	0.10445	0.10445	0.10445	0.10445
Profit	0.14311	0.14311	0.14311	0.14311	0.14311	0.14311	0.14311	0.14311	0.14311
Solvability	0.08578	0.08578	0.08578	0.08578	0.08578	0.08578	0.08578	0.08578	0.08578
Regular credit	0.24858	0.24858	0.24858	0.24858	0.24858	0.24858	0.24858	0.24858	0.24858
Regular placement	0.12746	0.12746	0.12746	0.12746	0.12746	0.12746	0.12746	0.12746	0.12746
Regular savings	0.19315	0.19315	0.19315	0.19315	0.19315	0.19315	0.19315	0.19315	0.19315
Sharia credits	0.03286	0.03286	0.03286	0.03286	0.03286	0.03286	0.03286	0.03286	0.03286
Sharia placements	0.03256	0.03256	0.03256	0.03256	0.03256	0.03256	0.03256	0.03256	0.03256
Sharia savings	0.03207	0.03207	0.03207	0.03207	0.03207	0.03207	0.03207	0.03207	0.03207

Sorong: West Papua

Limit SM	Liquidity	Profit	Solvability	Regular credit	Regular placements	Regular savings	Sharia credits	Sharia placements	Sharia savings
Liquidity	0.14669	0.14669	0.14669	0.14669	0.14669	0.14669	0.14669	0.14669	0.14669
Profit	0.12039	0.12039	0.12039	0.12039	0.12039	0.12039	0.12039	0.12039	0.12039
Solvability	0.06625	0.06625	0.06625	0.06625	0.06625	0.06625	0.06625	0.06625	0.06625
Regular credit	0.21026	0.21026	0.21026	0.21026	0.21026	0.21026	0.21026	0.21026	0.21026
Regular placement	0.23038	0.23038	0.23038	0.23038	0.23038	0.23038	0.23038	0.23038	0.23038
Regular savings	0.12525	0.12525	0.12525	0.12525	0.12525	0.12525	0.12525	0.12525	0.12525
Sharia credits	0.03315	0.03315	0.03315	0.03315	0.03315	0.03315	0.03315	0.03315	0.03315
Sharia placements	0.03059	0.03059	0.03059	0.03059	0.03059	0.03059	0.03059	0.03059	0.03059
Sharia savings	0.03254	0.03254	0.03254	0.03254	0.03254	0.03254	0.03254	0.03254	0.03254

References

Azis, I. J. (2018). Development and shortcomings of Indonesia's financial sector. In U. Volz, P. J. Morgan, & N. Yoshino (Eds.), *Routledge handbook of banking and finance in Asia*. Routledge.

Azis, I. J. (2024). *Listen and design: On micro, small and medium enterprises*. Springer.

Bernanke, B. S., & Gertler, M. (1995). Inside the black box: The credit channel of monetary policy transmission. *Journal of Economic Perspectives, 9*(4), 27–48.

Carlino, G., & DeFina, R. (1998). The differential regional effects of monetary policy. The Review of Economics and Statistics, 80(4).

Deloitte. (2024). Financial services authority (OJK) & Banking regulations update. *KM No. 3/May/2024*, 29 May.

Duran, H. E., & Erdem, U. (2014). Regional effects of monetary policy: Turkey case. *Regional and Sectoral Economic Studies, 14*(1).

Kashyap, A., & Jeremy, S. (1994). Monetary policy and bank lending. In *NBER studies in business cycles* (Vol. 29, pp. 221-256). NBER.

Pizzuto, P. (2020). Regional effects of monetary policy in the U.S.: An empirical re-assessment. *Economics Letters, 190.*

Romer, C. D., & Romer, D. H. (2004). A new measure of monetary shocks: Derivation and implications. *American Economic Review, 94*, 1055–1084.

Saaty, T. L. (2010). *Mathematical principles of decision making (Principia mathematica decernendi): The complete theory of the analytic hierarchy process*. RWS Publications.

Chapter 7
Reflections

Any process of development involves centripetal and centrifugal forces. In the physics of circular motion, centripetal forces keep an object moving in a circle and are always pointing toward the center of that circle. It is like the gravitational force of the Sun that keeps Earth orbiting it. In the economics of development, centripetal forces cause activities to concentrate in certain regions or locations (agglomeration phenomena), driven by the external economies. The opposite force, the centrifugal force, is fictitious. It is a phantom force but nevertheless feels very real, i.e., experiencing an outward force when we rotate the object in a circle. In spatial economics, this force refers to the dispersion of activities across regions. It is neither fictitious nor improbable.[1]

In physics, the effects of these two forces have an influence on numerous man-made activities. When a car travels a sharp curve, some degree of imbalance occurs. To counteract the centrifugal force that can cause an accident by pulling the car off the road, the friction between the tires and the road, as well as the driving speed and trajectory, can modify the intensity of the centripetal force needed to pull the car inward to bring it to safety. In economics, inequality caused by the interplay of the two forces is like the car imbalance. If growth with price stability is an analogy of car safety, monetary policy is like driving speed and the design of the road and tires. While the efficacy of the design to avoid accidence is determined by the severity of the car imbalance, the effectiveness of monetary policy to achieve the targets is affected by the degree of inequality.

[1] Both forces are actually the exact same force but just in opposite directions. The feeling or experience of it depends on our frames of reference. If we are looking from the viewpoint of the rotating object, we experience centrifugal force, but if we are outside the rotating system, we will observe centripetal force. The analogy in spatial economics could not be more obvious. In a crowded region like Jawa, massive inflows of people and activities are seen as the consequence of centripetal force, while if we look at the whole country, such can be seen as outward flows or 'talent exodus', spreading local resources away from outside Jawa to Jawa, mimicking the effect of centrifugal force.

I. J. Azis, *Monetary Whispers Across Space*,
https://doi.org/10.1007/978-981-95-4625-1_7

What is shown in the analysis throughout the book is that centripetal forces in Indonesia have been stronger than centrifugal forces. Even after some negative externalities emerged in the more developed regions, e.g., higher prices, congestion, etc., the concentration of activities persisted (sticky), causing a high degree of interregional inequality. Designed to maximize growth with price stability, monetary policy can exacerbate this inequality. In turn, inequality can reduce the effectiveness of monetary policy.

The evidence presented in Chap. 3 clearly indicates that despite the presence of numerous programs and policies to address the inequality between regions, Indonesia's interregional inequality is very high by international standards and has continued to worsen in recent years. More concerning is the inequality in productivity. Why does productivity matter more than GDP growth? Although income or GDP growth reflects short-term economic gains, productivity represents the engine of long-term development. Any GDP growth achieved in the short run cannot be sustained if productivity growth does not improve. This is because productivity encapsulates efficiency and innovation, laying the foundations for sustainable income improvements, competitiveness, and resilience. Higher productivity also reflects better environmental protection, an important part of sustainable development goals (SDG), i.e., to achieve the same level of output, a smaller amount of input is needed, hence less pollution and smaller resource depletion. Therefore, evaluating interregional inequality through the lens of productivity offers a more strategic perspective. It enables us to address the structural factors that allow economies to grow equitably across regions and adapt to evolving challenges. Elaborated in Chap. 3, the overall growth of productivity in Indonesia has been persistently declining and there was no sign of a decreasing trend in productivity inequality between regions.

The internal structure and inner mechanisms of Indonesia's structural transformation, in which dualism prevailed. have a lot to do with such a concerning trend. A normal pattern of development is known to refer to a decreasing share of agriculture and an increasing share of manufacturing and services in total production. On the surface, Indonesia appears to follow this pattern except that the share of manufacturing has been declining during the last few years (a sign of deindustrialization), causing a significant decline in the number of middle-class individuals from 57.3 million in 2019 to 47.8 million in 2024. But looking deeper into the implications on productivity, the sectoral shift has not been accompanied by the expected improvements in productivity. The country's structural transformation is anything but 'normal'.

The increasing prominence of the services sector has been marked by a sharp dualism. On the one hand, the trade sector, especially retail trade, which employs the majority of Indonesian workforce, has faced persistently low and declining productivity. However, modern services, including non labor-intensive industries such as information technology (IT) and sectors like finance, insurance, and real estate (FIRE), have much higher levels of productivity. Since the number of workers and the unit of operations in retail trade continued to increase, the overall growth of labor productivity declined. The trend paused during the first half of the last decade, but resumed in 2016. Ironically, this was the period when the country invested heavily in infrastructure and the use of digital technology spread rapidly. This disconnect between infrastructure expenditures and productivity performance raises concerns about the efficiency of capital allocation. It also suggests some potential misalignments in project selection, execution capacity, or complementary institutional reforms, undermining the catalytic potential of such investments.

Since centripetal forces were embedded in the development process and the inequality between regions remained high and still rising despite numerous policies that have been implemented, it is very likely that those policies were formulated without recognizing the strength and vigor of centripetal forces. Detecting these forces directly, let alone measuring them, is not easy. Instead, we tried to delineate what was involved in the system and what happened with the responses of different parts of the economy across regions when a policy shock was imposed.

Although the intraregional multipier made the increase in the region's output greater than the increase in spending, there were several transactions involved in the process; some were across sectors (increased production in one sector required input from other sectors) and some across regions (the required inputs were produced in other regions). Over the last few decades, numerous policies have been taken to increase spending in less developed regions outside Jawa. Yet, results of the calculation show that in general these policies failed to counter the strength and vigor of centripetal forces. The interregional inequality continues to be high and increasing (Chap. 3).

In many less developed regions outside Jawa, increasing output often required inputs and other supporting services from Jawa (regions in eastern Indonesia also imported them from Sulawesi). Hence, an increase in production outside Jawa generated an increase in income in Jawa, captured through interregional multipliers. Cross-regional effects also worked in the opposite direction when the initial increase of output occurred in Jawa. The question is which of the two was bigger? The discussions in Chap. 4 clearly indicate that the cross-regional benefits going towards Jawa were much bigger than those going to regions outside Jawa. This asymmetry in multipliers captured the elements of centripetal forces that had played an important role in causing a large development gap between developed and less developed regions.

To test the hypothesis that this high interregional inequality eroded the efficacy of monetary policy, we applied a mixed-effect model in Chap. 5. In an environment of high inequality, as in Indonesia, financial access tends to concentrate in only a few developed regions, that is, when the central bank raised money supply, the increased supply did not flow into a broad credit expansion. Some regions allocated credit disproportionately more than their economic size and conditions would suggest, while others allocated less. As the latter case exceeded the former, the overall regional credit allocation fell short of what would have been expected given the increase in the money supply. This partly explains why the credit/GDP ratio in Indonesia is very low (32% at the time of writing), the lowest among the major Southeast Asian countries.

Given the existing inequality, the largest share of the credit in many less developed regions went to the trade sector. But most of the goods that local consumers needed could not be produced in these regions due to their less developed infrastructure and status. As a result, a large share of the credits was spent elsewhere, mostly in more developed regions, suggesting that the initial gap between developed and less developed regions led to a credit allocation pattern that exacerbated the gap. In turn, this contributed to the limited effectiveness of monetary and credit policy. This two-way relationship is discussed in great detail in Chap. 2. If the cycle continues uninterrupted, the likelihood is high that Indonesia will retain its standing as one of the nations with the most pronounced interregional inequality, under which the effectiveness of the country's monetary policy would be further diminished.

There is a broader ramification of this. High interregional inequality can pose challenges to the formulation and effective implementation of national macroeconomic policies. When the interdependent and self-reinforcing process in a system created a cycle of negative outcomes that perpetuate themselves, formulating a policy intervention becomes difficult. The problems of inequality amplified the problems of ineffective monetary policy, and the latter amplified the problems of inequality. If the cycle becomes increasingly entrenched, not only will this cause inequality and ineffectiveness problems to get worse, but virtually any attempts to address one issue would be hindered by the persistence of others, thereby preventing escape from the cycle. Fiscal measures will fail to address the diverse needs of regions, and monetary policy will not function well; instead, it will exacerbate the gap between developed and less developed regions.

High inequality can also hinder the country's growth prospects as it creates an overall lag on the economy. When lagging regions (many in eastern Indonesia) remain stunted, the economy cannot harness the full potential, and resources tend to be distributed inefficiently, causing the underutilized potential of the less developed regions. When purchasing power in the less developed regions is weak, the growth opportunities of activities based on domestic demand will be limited, and if a large number of less developed regions with fewer resources continue to struggle to invest in education and healthcare, a large portion of the country's population is unable to fully contribute to the economy. These are in addition to the adverse consequences of high inequality on social and political instability that could deter investors and stall economic reforms necessary for future growth.

From any angle we look at it; therefore, problems caused by a large development gap between poor and rich regions should not be undermined. Until now, most existing policies have failed to narrow the gap. Counterbalancing the endogenous forces of agglomeration by addressing any institutional bottlenecks and ensuring compatibility with the prevailing social capital across regions would have been a much more effective approach to reduce interregional inequality in a country as diverse as Indonesia. Building infrastructure not aligned with local needs can lead to a number of adverse impacts, i.e. wasted and depleted resources, underutilization and inefficiency, missed opportunities for more impactful investments, unfulfilled potentials if the project cuts through valuable site such as protected forest or fertile land, destroyed ecosystem when it causes pollution, and creating social conflicts when the project disrupts the livelihood of local businesses, farmers, and communities.

While we are convinced with the above resolution, we also firmly believe that the behavior of local agents plays an important role in all these issues. In the context of our study, we pay particular attention to local banks. Their decisions on credit allocation as reflected in their day-to-day operations is very important to understand, and they can be used to verify the model-based conclusions as well as the appropriateness of certain indicators; e.g., loan-to-deposit ratio as a measure of liquidity preference.

From field surveys and in-depth discussions with local bankers in Jawa and outside Jawa, including eastern Indonesia, it was revealed that the behavior of local banks toward national monetary policy was heterogeneous. The responses to the policy varied according to the types of banks and the local conditions. Consistent with the relatively small loan-to-deposit ratio, most of the banks in Jawa had a strong liquidity preference. On the other hand, banks outside Jawa tend to focus more on profitability, except private banks (bank branches whose headquarters are in Jawa). This is also consistent with data showing a high loan-to-deposit ratio outside Jawa. Since the bank size is disproportionately larger in Jawa than in outside Jawa, the average ratio for the whole country is also relatively low (87% at the time of writing). On the question regarding the course of actions, smaller banks (especially rural banks or BPR) were of the opinion that improving their governance was most critical, while larger banks (state-owned and private) considered the adoption/improvement of digital technology to be the most needed course of actions. The details and other results of the survey are discussed in Chap. 6.

In further analysis of the results, there remain cases of inconsistency where local banks' perceptions did not align with the data on the loan-to-deposit ratio. Although the perceptions and day-to-day operations of some banks indicate a strong preference towards liquidity, the loan-to-deposit ratio data show otherwise. On the other hand, there were banks that kept a small loan-to-deposit ratio but expressed a stronger preference towards profitability than liquidity. Hence, the data do not always align with the true behaviors and perceptions of banks. This suggests that the loan-to-deposit ratio should be used with caution and may not be the best reference to use to assess the actual preference of banks for liquidity. Obtaining information directly from local banks is.

Upon further investigation, the source of the inconsistency was revealed. Many large (state-owned and private) banks in Jawa had more alternative investment options. They could allocate the deposit fund for assets other than credit, such as government bonds, equity, or other securities. They tend to be more proactive and aggressive in expanding their depositor base. In addition to causing the bank's loan-to-deposit ratio to be small, such behaviors also contributed to the low effectiveness of the central bank's monetary and credit policy. On the other hand, regions outside Jawa had a more limited and narrower financial market, giving banks no option but to allocate the deposit fund for credit. The only non-credit option they had was interbank placement in the form of saving or demand deposits in other banks just to earn some returns.

In summary, the interregional inequality in Indonesia was pronounced and continued to increase, creating a persistent imbalance between Jawa and non-Jawa and between eastern and western Indonesia. Most policies to reverse the trend failed to recognize the vigor and strength of centripetal forces, including institutional constraints and prevailing social capital. The high level of disparity in the country led to a pattern in which money supply-driven credit allocation in poorer regions often leaked and flowed outside the regions, further exacerbated the inequality. In turn, this dynamic weakened the effectiveness of monetary policy. If this self-reinforcing cycle is unattended, the effectiveness of monetary policy will be further diminished, and the adverse outcomes of inequality (sociopolitical-economic instability and missing growth opportunities) would be hard to avoid.

The problems of interregional inequality in Indonesia have been undermined for too long, creating a cynical and acrimonious atmosphere among analysts, policy makers, and local communities. We believe that these problems need to be openly laid out on the table and taken more seriously by policy makers, including monetary authority. The necessity of tackling interregional inequality reigns supreme and eclipses all other concerns. Recognizing that the money supply driven by monetary policy affects economic conditions in various locations in uneven ways is a necessary first step. Second guessing it is perilous, as it ignores 'Monetary Whispers Across Space'.

MIX
Papier aus verantwortungsvollen Quellen
Paper from responsible sources
FSC® C105338

If you have any concerns about our products,
you can contact us on
ProductSafety@springernature.com

In case Publisher is established outside the EU,
the EU authorized representative is:
Springer Nature Customer Service Center GmbH
Europaplatz 3, 69115 Heidelberg, Germany

Printed by Libri Plureos GmbH
in Hamburg, Germany